## "[A] REVEALING MEMOIR."
### —*The Hartford Courant*

"Sharp observations . . . Irving turns his skill with words to detailing the four directors, countless drafts, and serpentine negotiations on the journey from book to movie. . . . For someone whose novels are so skillfully, lovingly crafted, Irving shows a remarkable ability to let his literary children go. How does he do it? One line captures his spirit best: 'When I feel like being a director, I write a novel.'"

—*St. Louis Post-Dispatch*

"The beauty of *My Movie Business* is in the details. A lifelong wordsmith whose style of 'big' novels with social themes has been compared to that of Charles Dickens, Irving brings a unique perspective to the quirky ways of Holly-wood."

—*Ft. Worth Star Telegram*

"A fascinating, inside look at what it takes to turn a novel into a screenplay . . . Negotiations to include or exclude certain scenes, or to include or exclude directors, are detailed with panache. . . . A revealing glimpse into the creative process from one of America's most entertaining writers."

—*St. Petersburg Times*

"[An] eloquent memoir . . . [that] offers a fascinating and detailed look at how he trimmed his huge novel into a workable screenplay."

—*Publishers Weekly*

"Cineasts as well as Irving's fans ought to find this book enthralling whether they see the movie or not; those who see and like the movie shouldn't miss reading it."

—*Booklist*

"Insightful . . . Recommended . . . Humorously exploring the differences between writing novels and screenplays, Irving contemplates the movie world from the perspective of a fiction author."

—*Library Journal*

# MY MOVIE BUSINESS

MY

JOHN

MOVIE

IRVING

BUSINESS

A MEMOIR

BALLANTINE BOOKS • NEW YORK

A Ballantine Book
Published by The Random House Publishing Group

Copyright © 1999 by Garp Enterprises, Ltd.

Published in the United States by Ballantine Books, an imprint of The Random House Publishing Group, a division of Random House, Inc., New York.

Grateful acknowledgement is made to William Morrow and Company, Inc., for permission to reprint from *The Cider House Rules*, by John Irving, copyright © 1985 by Garp Enterprises, Ltd. Reprinted by permission of William Morrow and Company, Inc.

www.ballantinebooks.com

Library of Congress Catalog Card Number: 00-105869

ISBN: 0-345-44130-3

This edition published by arrangement with Random House, Inc.

Manufactured in the United States of America

Cover design by Honi Werner
Cover photograph by Stephen Vaughan/© Miramax Films

First Ballantine Books Edition: October 2000

9  8  7  6  5  4  3  2

*For my son Colin,*

*who has borne the disappointments*

*of this business with me.*

# CONTENTS

# MY MOVIE BUSINESS

# 1 | MRS. BERKELEY'S CONSTIPATION

y grandfather Dr. Frederick C. Irving gradu-
ated from Harvard Medical School in 1910.
He was an intern at the Massachusetts General
Hospital and later became chief of staff at the Boston
Lying-In—a pioneer institution, founded in 1832. In my
grandfather's day, the Boston Lying-In had already become
one of the world's leading obstetrical hospitals.

Dr. Irving was also a professor of obstetrics at Harvard,
and the author of three books: *The Expectant Mother's
Handbook, A Textbook of Obstetrics,* and a biography of the
Boston Lying-In Hospital called *Safe Deliverance.* The last
was chiefly a history of obstetrics and gynecological
surgery in the United States; it was published in 1942, the
year I was born. When I first told my parents that I wanted
to become a writer—I was fourteen—my parents said,

"Well, your grandfather is a writer. You should read his books."

And so, at about the same time I first read Charles Dickens, I began to read my grandfather "Fritz" Irving. For a fourteen-year-old, the clinical details of the early days of obstetrics and gynecological surgery were frankly more eye-opening than anything in Charles Dickens, although Dickens would ultimately prove to be a greater influence on my writing than Dr. Irving. Thank goodness.

My grandfather was an unusual physician—a man of science, but with Renaissance knowledge and positively Victorian prose. A short example of the latter should suffice.

A student of medicine begins his novitiate when he goes to medical school; but he should have entered upon his apprenticeship as a doctor many years before, when for the first time he was allowed free choice in his earlier education. At that point two roads are always open: one, straight and narrow, that leads through the sciences with only a few brief detours into general knowledge; the other, circuitous and serpentine, that wanders far afield, dips more deeply into the wider realms of learning, and returns to the highway only when necessity demands— this is the more entrancing road, for there are more flowers beside it, and from the ancient hills that it surmounts one sees the world more clearly.

It was clear to me, from an early age, that I would be a traveler on exclusively the circuitous and serpentine road—the one with more flowers beside it. Medical school was not for me. I wasn't a good enough student. Yet the only author I actually knew was a renowned obstetrician with a questionable sense of humor.

Well, maybe that isn't true. One summer in New Hampshire, on the beach at Little Boars Head, when I was still a young boy, someone pointed to a pale, ungainly man in a yellow bathing suit and said: "That's Ogden Nash, the writer." To this day I don't know if it was, but I shall carry the image of that funny-looking man, "the writer," to my grave. I immediately took up reading Ogden Nash's humorous verse, although I never thought that Mr. Nash's sense of humor could hold a candle to my grandfather's.

In introducing one of his patients to the reader, Grandfather wrote: "Mrs. Berkeley had contributed nothing to the world except her constipation." That would be a fine first sentence to a novel. I'm sorry my grandfather didn't write novels, for his sense of humor was not limited to his medical writings. He was also the author of a scandalous poem called "The Ballad of Chambers Street"; it is a poem of such astonishing lewdness and vulgarity that I will not repeat more than two stanzas. There are seventeen stanzas in all, four of which are anti-Semitic; another four are deeply obscene. But just so you can appreciate the sound

of the thing, here are two of the least offensive stanzas.
(The poem concerns the unwanted pregnancy of a loose
young woman named Rose who has a catastrophic abortion. The procedure is performed by an abortionist named
Charlie Green. The real Dr. Green was a respected professor of obstetrics and gynecology at Harvard.)

> High in a suite in Chambers Street,
> ere yet her waters broke,
> From pregnant Rose they took her clothes
> and ne'er a word they spoke.
> They laid her head across the bed,
> her legs they had to bend 'em.
> With sterile hands they made demands
> to open her pudendum.

> "The introitus admits my fist
> without the slightest urgin'.
> Therefore I ween," said Charlie Green,
> "that Rose is not a virgin.
> And I would almost dare declare
> that she has had coition,
> which in the main would best explain
> her present sad condition."

For years after my grandfather's death, my father
would receive handwritten and typewritten copies of the
infamous ballad; Dr. Irving's medical-school students

had faithfully transcribed "The Ballad of Chambers Street" from memory. Medical students have excellent memories.

Grandfather was a man of extreme erudition and unaccountable, even inspired, bad taste; as such, he would have been a terrific novelist, for a good novel is at once sophisticated in its understanding of human behavior and utterly rebellious in its response to the conventions of good taste.

As Charlotte Brontë wrote in 1847: "Conventionality is not morality. Self-righteousness is not religion. To attack the first is not to assail the last." I used the Brontë quotation as an epigraph to my sixth novel, *The Cider House Rules,* together with a far more prosaic observation made by a physician named H. J. Boldt in 1906. "For practical purposes abortion may be defined as the interruption of gestation before viability of the child."

Grandfather probably agreed with Dr. Boldt. Notwithstanding the Hippocratic oath—*Primum non nocere* ("First do no harm")—a physician existed "for practical purposes."

But Fritz Irving also had a fondness for mischief. He admired a colleague who once noted that many Irish women got pregnant on St. Patrick's Day. When they were ready to be delivered, Grandfather's colleague gave them a small dose of methylene blue—a harmless drug that colored their urine green, which the Irish women took as a sign of safe deliverance from St. Patrick himself.

## 2 | THE ETHER ADDICT

The plot of *The Cider House Rules* is far more complicated than the compressed version of the story and
its characters that I adapted as a screenplay (over a
thirteen-year period, and for four different directors). In
the novel, I began with the four failed adoptions of the orphan Homer Wells. By the end of the first chapter, when
Homer returns for the fourth time to the orphanage in St.
Cloud's, Maine, the orphanage physician, Dr. Wilbur
Larch, decides he'll have to keep him.

Dr. Larch, an obstetrician and (in the 1930s and '40s)
an illegal abortionist, trains Homer Wells to be a doctor.
This is illegal, too, of course—Homer never goes to high
school or to college, not to mention medical school. But
with Dr. Larch's training and the assistance of Larch's

faithful nurses, Angela and Edna, Homer becomes an experienced obstetrician and gynecologist. He refuses to perform abortions, however.

The second chapter of the novel describes Larch's childhood and medical-school years, his first internship in Boston, and the experiences that have made him "a patron saint of orphans" and an abortionist. The history of Homer's failed adoptions and Larch's background are not developed in the screenplay. Larch's ether addiction *is* developed in both the book and the film, but his sexual abstemiousness, a feature of his eccentricity in the novel, was never in any draft of the script; instead, in the movie, I strongly imply that Dr. Larch may have had (or still has) a sexual relationship with Nurse Angela.

I wanted to make Larch more normal. There is less time for character development in a film than in a novel; a character's eccentricities can too easily *become* the character. In the movie, I thought Larch's addiction to ether was eccentric enough.

In the screenplay, as in the novel, it is both Homer's conflict with Larch over the abortion issue *and* Homer's desire to see something of the world outside St. Cloud's that make him leave the orphanage with Wally Worthington and Candy Kendall—an attractive couple who come to St. Cloud's for an abortion. But in the book, Homer spends fifteen years away from the orphanage—in that time, Wally and Homer become best friends, Homer falls in love with Candy, and Wally and Candy get married.

The passage of time, which is so important in all my novels, is not easily captured in a film. In the screenplay, Homer stays away from St. Cloud's for only fifteen *months,* Wally *isn't* Homer's best friend, and Candy is the sexual aggressor in her relationship with Homer.

And in the novel, Homer and Candy have a son, Angel, who they pretend is adopted. Wally, out of love for all of them, tolerates this obvious fiction and his wife's infidelity. In the screenplay, there is no child and Wally never knows about Candy's transgressions. Developing sympathy, not unlike developing character, takes time; in the movie, I tried to make Homer more sympathetic by making him less responsible for the affair with Candy. I made less of the affair, too.

But in both the novel and the screenplay, what precipitates Homer's return to the orphanage, where he replaces Dr. Larch as the obstetrician *and* the abortionist in St. Cloud's, is his discovery of the relationship between a black migrant apple picker and his daughter. Mr. Rose, the picking-crew boss on the apple farm where Wally gives Homer a job, impregnates his own daughter, Rose Rose. In the novel, it is Homer and Candy's son, Angel, who falls in love with Rose Rose and first makes this discovery, but since I eliminated Angel from the screenplay, I made Homer find out about Rose Rose's pregnancy directly.

When Homer acknowledges that he must perform an abortion on Rose Rose, he realizes that he can no longer deny that procedure to other women who want it. All the time Homer Wells is away from St. Cloud's, the aging and ether-addicted Dr. Larch has been plotting how Homer can replace him; in the end of both the novel and the film, Homer accepts the responsibility Larch has left to him. The doctor's young apprentice becomes the orphanage physician.

Left out of the movie was the book-length character of Melony, an older girl who befriends Homer as a young orphan at St. Cloud's. Melony is also the source of Homer's sexual initiation, and she extracts from him a promise he will break—that he won't leave her. But I eliminated her from the screenplay; she was simply too overpowering a character.

Over and over again, the limitation imposed on the length of a movie has consequences. The novel of *The Cider House Rules* was more than 800 manuscript pages long— it's more than 500 book pages. The finished screenplay was a mere 136 manuscript pages. It pained me to lose Melony, but I had to do it.

It helped me that there'd been a precedent to losing Melony. In several foreign countries where the novel was translated, I lost the *title*. (Of my nine novels, *The Cider House Rules* is my favorite title.) In some languages, *The Cider House Rules* was simply too clumsy to translate. In

France, cider is an alcoholic drink; in German, "cider house rules" is one word. I forget what the problem was in Finnish, but the Finns titled the novel *The Hero of His Own Life*—from the beginning of *David Copperfield,* which Dr. Larch reads and rereads to the orphans at St. Cloud's. Homer Wells takes the opening passage from *David Copperfield* personally. "Whether I shall turn out to be the hero of my own life, or whether that station will be held by anybody else, these pages must show."

The German title, *Gottes Werk und Teufels Beitrag* (*The Work of the Lord, the Contribution of the Devil*), imitates Dr. Larch's manner of speaking in code to his nurses. (The French made a similar choice for the title: *L'Oeuvre de Dieu, la Part du Diable.*) This is Larch's way of indicating to Angela and Edna whether he is delivering a baby or performing an abortion. The point being that, in Larch's view, it is *all* the Lord's work—either he is delivering a baby or he is delivering a mother. (In the film, Dr. Larch's willingness to give abortions is established in the montage over the opening credits. Homer's reluctance to perform the procedure is expressed in the first scene of dialogue between them.)

I felt that a man who takes on the enormous responsibility of life or no life in an orphanage in poor, rural Maine—a man like Dr. Larch—would be deeply scarred. For this reason I made Larch an ether addict.

Ether was first synthesized in 1540 by a twenty-five-year-old Prussian botanist. People have been having ether frolics—and later, laughing-gas parties—ever since. In the proper hands, ether remains one of the safest inhalation agents known. At a concentration of only 1 or 2 percent, it is a light, tasty vapor; some forty years ago, hundreds of cases of cardiac surgery were done with ether and partially awake (even talking) patients.

Some of Dr. Larch's colleagues would have preferred nitrous oxide or chloroform, but Larch developed his preference for ether through self-administration. You would have to be crazy to self-administer chloroform. It is twenty-five times more toxic to the heart muscle than is ether, and it has an extremely narrow margin of safety; a minimal overdose can result in cardiac irregularity and death.

Nitrous oxide requires a very high (at least 80 percent) concentration to do the job, and it is always accompanied by a degree of what is called hypoxia—insufficient oxygen. It requires careful monitoring and cumbersome apparatus, and the patient runs the risk of bizarre fantasies or giggling fits. Induction is very fast. Coleridge was a laughing-gas man, although the poet was certainly familiar with ether, too. It was unfortunate for Coleridge that he preferred opium. Ether is a kinder drug addiction to bear. But no drug addiction is without risk—and no self-administered anesthesia is safe. After all, in both the novel and the film, Dr. Larch accidentally kills himself with ether.

When I first thought about the grounding for Dr.

Larch's character, I kept one principle foremost in mind: he goes to extremes. In the novel, he has sex just once, with a prostitute who gives him gonorrhea. He starts taking ether to numb himself to the pain of the gonococci; by the time the bacteria burns itself out, Larch is addicted to the ether. I thought that he should be no less extreme as a doctor.

In the movie, Larch's onetime experience with the prostitute, his case of the clap, and his subsequent sexual abstemiousness are gone. What remains is his ether addiction; without a history, it seems more desperate, more extreme. Homer defends Larch's reasons for taking ether by saying that Larch needs it to help him sleep ("He's too tired to sleep"), but the ether numbs Larch's overall pain. He takes it to relieve his angst, his *Weltschmerz*.

My grandfather's predecessor—the founding father of the Boston Lying-In, Dr. Walter Channing—was the first physician to use ether to relieve the pains of childbirth. Thus Dr. Channing became the founding father of obstetric anesthesia in America. Dr. Channing was one of my grandfather's heroes, just as one of Dr. Channing's heroes was the great Benjamin Rush. It was Rush who wrote that "pain does not accompany child-bearing by an immutable decree from Heaven."

But in Dr. Irving's day, there were still those obstetricians and midwives who believed that pain was a necessary, even a sacred part of the birthing process. The popular return of midwifery in the United States today, and the practice of so-called natural childbirth—indeed, the disdain for making any kind of anesthesia a part of the childbearing process—would doubtless have been greeted with contempt by my grandfather, who saw nothing "natural" (not to mention "sacred") in a mother's pain in childbirth, and who was old enough to remember when male physicians in obstetrics were looked upon with abhorrence.

"Those days of false modesty," Grandfather called them, "when females had limbs rather than legs; and pelvic examinations, if made at all, were often conducted under a sheet, which only increased the uncertainty already existing in the mind of the doctor." Like Dr. Larch, Dr. Frederick C. Irving was used to being in conflict—not only with prudish public opinion but also with his more conservative brother practitioners.

M y father, Colin Franklin Newell Irving, is named after another mentor of my grandfather's, Dr. Franklin Newell, who pioneered the change from the antiseptic to the aseptic technique at the Boston Lying-In Hospital, introducing the use of rubber gloves in 1903. Before then, even when physicians washed their hands, a death rate of about one in thirty (among obstetrical patients at lying-in hospitals) was regarded as standard—and, in Grandfather's words, "accepted almost with equanimity." It was of the utmost importance, my grandfather wrote, to rescue obstetrics from what he called "the relics of barbarism."

Prenatal clinics were established at the Boston Lying-In in 1911; to cite only the example of eclampsia and eclamptic convulsions, the frequency of eclamptic patients requiring treatment immediately fell to a quarter of its former rate.

The first cesarean section to be performed at the Boston Lying-In Hospital was on July 13, 1894. The procedure required forty-six minutes. An incision was made in the abdominal wall, almost a foot long, and the uterus was lifted through it—"an enormous organ," as my grandfather has described it, "the color of a ripe plum." The uterus rested on the patient's abdomen, where it was said (in my grandfather's words) "to fill the eyes of the beholders with wonder and respect."

Grandfather describes the exposed uterus, in such a procedure, as follows: "A quick slash through its walls brought a gush of liquid and blood which shot halfway across the room." He adds: "The operation as performed today [he meant the 1940s] is a comparatively dull affair; the incision is much smaller and the uterus is opened as it lies in the abdominal cavity. Much of the drama has gone."

When I began my research for *The Cider House Rules,* I needed to see a bowel-cancer surgery in order to appreciate what a cesarean section in the old days must have looked like.

As for abortion, Grandfather was wise to observe that "as long as there are unwanted pregnancies, women will attempt to rid themselves of them." I was fourteen when I read that, in 1956. I was forty-three when *The Cider House Rules* was published, in 1985. I like to think that my grandfather would have enjoyed the novel. I doubt that the story of the good Dr. Larch becoming an abortionist would have shocked him. That part of the story, I believe, would have merited Dr. Irving's approval.

There is another part of the novel, however, of which I'm certain Grandfather would have *dis*approved. That Dr. Larch must find a young abortionist to replace him was a necessary reality of orphanage hospitals that I doubt Dr.

Irving ever considered. It would probably have offended my grandfather's sense of proper training even to imagine that Dr. Larch would need to *create,* among the best and the brightest of his unadoptable orphans, a fellow obstetrician and abortionist.

After all, Fritz Irving was a Harvard man. The concept of a single physician training a mere boy to be a doctor—not to mention creating false credentials for his young medical student, which Dr. Larch does—would not likely have gained my grandfather's sympathy. More likely, as much a pioneer in his field as he was, Dr. Irving was old-school in the sense that he believed in schools. He believed in the tradition of medicine (despite its aforementioned "relics of barbarism"); he believed in the idea of a curriculum of training for physicians. Medicine was a frontier for my grandfather, but a formal education and its boundaries were the gods he believed in.

Dr. Irving would not have wanted Dr. Larch to go to jail, or to lose his license to practice medicine, simply because he performed abortions; however, I'm guessing that Grandfather *would* have wanted Homer Wells to go to jail for being less than a properly trained physician. Moreover, Dr. Frederick C. Irving was never a fan of midwives. Had he been alive to read my novel, I've little doubt that Grandfather would have deemed Homer no better than a glorified midwife.

Yet I took great pains in *The Cider House Rules* to make Dr. Larch a good teacher and Homer Wells a dutiful student. Homer makes no mistakes of a medical nature in the novel—nor, to my knowledge, did I. A medical historian read the book in manuscript, as did several doctors, an obstetrician and gynecological surgeon among them. (I was told sarcastically by one of the doctors that I somehow managed to get my episiotomies in the right place.)

In the course of researching the novel, I saw a number of babies born, a number of abortions performed, and a number of other gynecological procedures of a surgical kind. I never fainted or threw up, but the bowel-cancer surgery made me sweat. At one point—when the patient, although fully anesthetized, opened her eyes and appeared to stare at her insides, which were piled on top of her abdomen (not inside her, where they belonged) . . . well, at *that* point I felt I couldn't get sufficient air through my surgical mask.

"She's awake!" I whispered to the anesthesiologist, who appeared to be asleep.

He calmly looked at the patient and said, "Close your eyes, dear," which she did.

Later the anesthesiologist told me: "There are *degrees* of what you novelists call 'awake.'"

Given the sophistication of modern medicine, we forget how recent much of this is. Anesthesia, antibiotics, an understanding of sepsis—all are recent. Even more recent is a substantial increase in the general public's comprehension of hygiene. People today have more medical common sense. But when my grandfather was a young intern in the South End of Boston, his principal patients were poor immigrants, many of them living in cold-water slums. "All the standard forms of vice were there," Grandfather wrote, "such as prostitution, drug addiction, and alcoholism; and in addition palmists, fortune-tellers, Chinese herb doctors, abortionists, and sexual perverts were all about."

As a young obstetrician, Fritz Irving made many home

deliveries. He carried a bag with a small sterilizer containing rubber gloves, two clamps, a pair of scissors for cutting the umbilical cord, and a bottle of ergot to make the uterus contract after delivery. He once delivered a Lithuanian child near Haymarket Square. The baby was born normally, but the afterbirth refused to come away. The new mother's mother, who was attending the birth, gave her daughter a beer bottle to blow into. This sometimes worked—by increasing the intra-abdominal pressure. But the beer-bottle method failed this time. As the young woman was bleeding freely, my grandfather knew that unless he delivered the afterbirth promptly, he would be faced with a serious hemorrhage.

Grandfather grasped the top of the new mother's uterus through her abdominal wall and squeezed firmly. His patient screamed and clawed at his hands. The patient's mother seized him around the waist (in an attempt to bite him in the back). The patient's husband, also in attendance, tried to strangle my grandfather. But the placenta separated and soon appeared, just as Grandfather felt he was near to fainting. "The family," Dr. Irving wrote, "balked of their opportunity to do me bodily injury, lapsed into sulky silence."

Perhaps it was experiences like these that gave my grandfather a condescending view of the poor and the uneducated, and of the many ethnic minorities in the South

End of Boston in his time. I remember him (maybe falsely) as an imperious and scornful figure, usually in a three-piece suit; a gold pocket watch made his vest pocket bulge. He wore suspenders and cufflinks. The smell of ether surrounded him like a shroud. (Probably I have imagined the ether—the smell of which, from my tonsillectomy, is as permanent as certain childhood nightmares.)

At Harvard Medical School in Dr. Irving's day, all the Boston hospitals—possibly because there were so many of them—were known by their nicknames or abbreviations. The Peter Bent Brigham Hospital was called the Peter Bent; the Boston Lying-In was the B.L.I. My grandfather, even for years after he retired from the medical-school faculty, was known as The Great God Irving of the B.L.I.

But, in his own family, no one dared follow Fritz Irving into medicine. Had he cut too daunting a path? Our failure to follow in his footsteps could conceivably have disappointed him. I don't really know—I never knew him well. Grandfather died of a heart attack on Christmas Eve, 1957, when I was fifteen.

Now many (if not most) of his former medical-school students are also dead. I hear more frequently from some of the grown children that my grandfather delivered; most of them are older than I am. Since they were only newborn babies when they first and last laid eyes on my grandfather, they have no idea that he was once known as The Great

God Irving of the B.L.I. All they know about him is that he wrote that highly objectionable poem, which their parents have handed down to them; since the publication of *The Cider House Rules,* some of them have sent me handwritten or typewritten copies. (Now, instead of my father, *I* am sent copies of the scandalous poem.)

Once a retired obstetrician called me and recited all seventeen stanzas of "The Ballad of Chambers Street" from memory over the telephone. He was calling from a restaurant in Florida. He was drunk, but lucidly drunk. It was his grandson's wedding, he said; everyone was giving speeches. When it was the retired doctor's turn to speak, "The Ballad of Chambers Street" came back to him in its entirety. After he'd recited the poem to the astonished wedding party, his wife banished him from the table. Then he called me.

"But my phone number is unlisted," I said to him. (I was living in New York City at the time.) "How'd you get my phone number?"

He replied that, as a doctor, he'd had "fair success" at getting calls put through to people with unlisted phone numbers. "It works about half the time," he assured me.

"*What* works?" I asked him.

"I say I'm calling to report a death in the family," the old doctor told me. "The key is overwhelming the operator with a lot of medical language."

I suppose that a retired obstetrician who could remember "The Ballad of Chambers Street" from his days in medical school could be reasonably "overwhelming."

I thanked the elderly gentleman for his phone call. "Dr. Irving would have been proud of you," I added.

I know a man (I'm sure you do, too) who has the irritating habit of saying, repeatedly, "That sounds like something that could happen only in a novel." Well, here is yet another entry in that ever-expanding category: one of America's pioneers in obstetrics and gynecological surgery is best remembered for a dirty poem. As my dad said to me once: "What your grandfather wrote in one weekend has already outlived him, and his reputation, by almost forty years."

n 1980, when I first wrote some notes to myself about *The Cider House Rules,* I began with the imagined relationship between an orphanage physician and an unadoptable orphan—a child he brings into the world who cannot find a place *in* the world. Each time the orphan is adopted, it doesn't work; he ends up back at the orphanage. The physician, a childless man, becomes like a father to this boy. But if they know the love of a father-son relationship, they also know the conflict. When I began my notes on the novel, I didn't know what the conflict would be—only that there had to be one.

I went to the medical-history library at Yale. The more I read about orphanages and orphanage hospitals, the more I realized that, in that period of time when abortion was illegal in the United States (between 1846 and 1973), a woman with an unwanted pregnancy would be more likely to find a physician willing to give her a safe abortion in an orphanage hospital than in any other kind. A doctor in an orphanage would know what happened, and what too often *didn't* happen, to those children who were left behind. In Dr. Larch's day, there were many orphans—most notably, the sickly and the unattractive—languishing in orphanages, unadopted. In their teenage years, they would become wards of the state.

And so I made Dr. Larch an abortionist. As for the young orphan he trains to be a doctor, I made Homer Wells unwilling to perform abortions. After all, he's an orphan—the only thing his mother gave him was life itself. Homer feels lucky to be alive. This, I decided, would be the conflict that would drive Dr. Larch and his beloved orphan apart. Homer will learn how to perform an abortion, but he won't want to. For fifteen years, he'll refuse.

*The Cider House Rules* is a didactic novel. The nature of Dr. Larch's argument with Homer Wells is polemical, and Larch wins the argument in the end. Larch is a polemicist raving against an entrenched moral doctrine of his day. That abortions are illegal doesn't stop Dr. Larch from providing them—nor, as I've said, is this the only law Larch breaks. He lovingly creates college and medical-school degrees for Homer; indeed, the falsification of these documents gives Larch inordinate pleasure.

In my screenplay of *The Cider House Rules*—but not in

the novel—I have Nurse Angela object that Homer's credentials are against the law. (So much of the *argument* of the novel is carried on in the narration; the characters' thoughts are often internal, not expressed. In the film, the dialogue best advances the argument that drives the story.)

"We all know who trained Homer—his credentials are as good as mine are," Larch tells Angela. "Don't you be holy to me about the law. What has the law done for any of us here?"

"I don't want to perform abortions," Homer says to Larch. "I have no argument with *you* performing them."

Larch replies: "You know *how* to help these women—how can you not feel obligated to help them when they can't get help anywhere else?"

"I didn't ask to know how—you just showed me," Homer protests.

"What *else* could I have shown you, Homer?" Larch argues. "The only thing I can teach you is what I know."

The first chapter of the novel is titled "The Boy Who Belonged to St. Cloud's." (It was my earliest title for the book.) The point is, Homer Wells will never get away from what Larch has taught him.

"I expect you to be of use," Larch tells the boy.

"For Homer Wells, this was easy," I wrote at the end of the first chapter. "*Of use,* he felt, was all that an orphan was born to be."

Larch's edict "to be of use" is strictly in keeping with his utilitarian nature. Homer, like any young man, wants to live his own life—like any boy, he wants to have an adventure or two.

Homer has far fewer adventures in the movie of *The Cider House Rules* than I permit him to have in the book. What was, to begin with, a didactic novel is no less didactic as a film, but Homer has less fun.

Larch's argument with Homer dominates the screenplay. It *should,* although it may not necessarily, dominate the movie. (I'll leave that judgment to the audience. I'm unsure of the final result because Larch's lengthiest and most bitter argument with Homer didn't survive the director's first cut of the film.) While a woman's right to an abortion, and all that that implies, is the dominant argument of the book, in the necessary compression of the story—to make a long, plot-driven novel into a feature-length film—the distillation of Larch's polemics becomes stronger stuff in the script. Maybe *too* strong. Michael Caine's choice, which was to play Larch *softly,* helps to quiet how loud Larch is on the page.

While the Homer of the novel is a passive hero who seizes control of his own life and dedicates himself to Larch's cause only upon his mentor's death and as a result of the drag-on fifteen-year affair with his best friend's wife, the Homer of the movie seems *more* passive—

because Caine-as-Larch is *less* of a moral bully than Larch is in the book.

When I saw the director's first cut of the film, I thought there were a few too many close-ups of Homer. For much of the film, until he makes up his mind to perform the abortion on Rose Rose and return to St. Cloud's, the expressions on Homer's face are his *only* responses to the world—both inside and outside the orphanage. In the movie, Homer's expressions are perfect—meaning utterly true to his character—but I cautioned the director that too many close-ups of his keenly observant but inactive expressions served to underline his passivity. So much of the novel was missing from the screenplay, I didn't want the movie audience to grow tired of Homer's lack of action before he becomes an active hero.

Missing from the screenplay, too, are most of the novel's scenes of comic relief. Despite the abortion polemic, *The Cider House Rules*—like all my novels—is a comic novel. There is little "relief" of any kind in the screenplay, wherein the grim and difficult-to-accept truth of Dr. Larch's utilitarian message is given center stage. The screenplay condenses the novel in such a way that the story's harshest elements stand out all the harsher in their relative isolation.

Candy's betrayal of Wally seems *more* of a betrayal. Homer seems more needed at St. Cloud's, and Larch seems more impatient to get him to come back. Larch's ether habit is more lugubrious. And all the deaths are more truncated in film time—Fuzzy's death, the death of the unnamed twelve-year-old who has the botched abortion, the violent end of Mr. Rose, and Larch's tired succumbing to ether.

"Even for me," chirps little Jane Eyre, "life had its gleams of sunshine." Not in this orphan story, not as a film. In the screenplay, I made a decision to hold the "sunshine"; I thought there was no time for sunshine. (The director, Lasse Hallström, persuaded me to interject a *little* sunshine into my final draft of the screenplay; it's a good thing he did. Now the producer, Richard Gladstein, says: "While we don't have the brightest of movies, there is a *bit* of sunshine here and there." I concede that he's right.)

In the screenplay, I have the ever-thoughtful Buster ask Larch what the twelve-year-old girl died of. Larch won't say "a botched abortion," but he says everything else. Pounding the dead girl's coffin, he rails at Buster. "She died of *secrecy,* she died of *ignorance* . . ."

"It's bad luck to hit a coffin," Buster interrupts him.

"She died of *superstition,* too!" Larch shouts. (I think I had Larch bully Buster too much. In the first rough cut of the movie, Lasse edited out Buster's line about hitting a coffin and Larch's rejoinder about superstition.)

There is no Buster in the book. I created him to stand as

a replacement of Homer as a younger boy, because I didn't have the time to reproduce Homer's childhood in the screenplay. (One of the film's co-producers, and Lasse Hallström's longtime creative partner, Leslie Holleran, made many valuable contributions to the script; Leslie suggested that it would be a good idea to see a *little* of Homer's childhood, if only in montage over the opening credits. She was right.)

I've already said why I eliminated Melony from the screenplay. She would have overpowered Homer—she almost overpowers him in the novel. In the film, she might have rivaled even Dr. Larch. I wanted no one, not even Mr. Rose, to rival Larch.

Movies are not only popular with nonreaders; they are also for young people and for restless readers. Doubtless many moviegoers will "identify" with Homer Wells. For most of the audience—the younger members, especially—Homer will be the main character, but Dr. Larch is the most important character to me.

My friend Peter Matthiessen read the novel *The Cider House Rules* in manuscript. He said that I should make Larch the main character; Peter urged me to revise the novel, taking some scenes away from Homer, giving more to Larch. I agreed with Peter, and tried to heed his criticism, but I was not entirely successful. *The Cider House Rules* is a novel with *two* main characters.

I'm not saying that novels with two main characters are necessarily flawed, but they create problems of focus—for both their authors and their readers. *The World According to Garp* is also such a novel; Garp may be the principal main character, but his mother, Jenny Fields, is a much more dramatic character than he is. Many readers wrote me that they wanted Jenny to be the main character.

In writing the screenplay of *The Cider House Rules,* I felt I was given the opportunity to make Dr. Larch the uncontested main character of the film. This idea was met with formidable resistance; all four directors associated with the project wanted more of Homer and less of Larch. The result is that Homer is in many more scenes. In movie language, Homer is the star of the picture. Nonetheless I am hopeful that Dr. Larch is the driving force behind the film, even when he's not on camera.

*The Cider House Rules* is a symbolic title. To anyone familiar with the story, *Larch's* rules are the rules that apply.

set *The Cider House Rules* in Maine because it was the first state in the country to make abortion illegal. From colonial times, abortion had always been permitted until the fetus was "quick"; in other words, until the fetus was advanced enough to make movement of its own that could be differentiated from the mother's movement. Thus, in the first trimester of pregnancy, abortion was legal in the United States, even in the time of the Puritans. Notwithstanding the punitive beliefs of America's deeply religious founding fathers, abortion was nobody's business but the woman's herself.

Later, in the state of Maine, the Eastman-Everett Act of 1840 declared that performing an abortion was punishable by a year in jail or a $1,000 fine, or both. If you were a doctor, you might also lose your license to practice. By

1846, abortion was illegal throughout the United States; it remained so until 1973, when the *Roe* v. *Wade* Supreme Court decision held that a woman had a constitutional right to an abortion. Exactly what happened to make the procedure illegal for 127 years when, for the first 226 years—since the pilgrims landed at Plymouth Rock—it had been legal?

Ironically, doctors were the first to undermine a woman's right to an abortion. In the 1830s, a group of doctors in the American Medical Association believed that midwives were making too much money performing abortions; it was money that the doctors believed *they* should be making instead. They argued that performing an abortion was a lot more difficult, medically, than delivering a child, so only doctors should perform the procedure. Yet for years midwives had been doing abortions with as great a degree of safety as had doctors.

As for the greater danger, between childbirth and abortions in the 1830s, women who were having their babies at lying-in hospitals ran a far greater risk of dying from childbed fever (puerperal fever) than women delivering babies *or* having abortions at home. As my grandfather wrote: "In cases where those in labor and those recently delivered were bedded in a proximity that afforded facilities for the transfer of infection from one to the other, puerperal fever attained the proportion of a pestilence."

By 1840, nevertheless, a group of doctors had managed

to take abortion out of the hands of midwives; and once the only legal access to the procedure rested with doctors, *another* group of doctors (but not entirely a different group) within the American Medical Association lobbied for the procedure to be declared illegal.

This is as confusing as it is contradictory. But, in retrospect, many doctors were unprepared to discover that midwives had been as busy performing abortions as delivering babies. The doctors panicked. At first they had wanted the money that midwives were making from performing abortions. But then, when some of these same doctors recognized how overwhelming the need for abortion was, they wanted nothing to do with it.

I will never fully comprehend this murky history, but at least one book from the period is clear. It was published in New York in 1860—Mrs. W. H. Maxwell's *A Female Physician to the Ladies of the United States.* Mrs. Maxwell treated "all diseases peculiar to women, or which they may have unfortunately incurred through the dissipations or wanton unfaithfulness of husbands, or otherwise." (In short, she treated venereal diseases.) Mrs. Maxwell also wrote that she gave her attention, as well, "to women . . . who are forced by the malfunction of their genital organs, or other cause, to resort to premature delivery." (In short, she performed abortions.)

Until the late 1870s, Mrs. Maxwell operated a women's

clinic in New York. "The authoress has not established her hospital simply for the benefit of lying-in women," she wrote. "She believes that in view of the uncharitableness of general society towards the erring, it is fit that the unfortunate should have some sanctuary to which to flee, in whose shade they may have undisturbed opportunity to reflect, and hiding forever their present unhappiness, nerve themselves to be wiser in the future. The true physician's soul cannot be too broad and gentle."

Mrs. Maxwell was one of my earliest models for Dr. Larch. Larch's soul could not be too broad and gentle, I decided; yet, with Homer, Larch is ruthless. Larch may be Homer's physician, but he is primarily Homer's father, and he is Homer's teacher. Larch starts training Homer to be his replacement when Homer is just a boy.

As for what Mrs. Maxwell accurately describes as "the uncharitableness of general society towards the erring," I am reminded of an expression that was more common in my grandfather's day, which was also Dr. Larch's day, than it is nowadays, although the spirit behind this expression is still present. It was what people used to say about a young, unmarried girl who got pregnant: "She is paying the piper."

# 8 | BUT COULD IT REALLY BE TAUGHT TO A CHIMPANZEE?

Think of the Right-to-Life movement today. It is fueled by something stronger than a concern for the rights of the unborn. (Proponents of the Right-to-Life position show very little concern for children once they're born.) What underlies the Right-to-Life message is a part of this country's fundamental sexual puritanism. Right-to-Lifers believe that what *they* perceive as promiscuity should not go unpunished; girls who get pregnant should pay the piper.

This thinking is more invasive than many other manifestations of invasion of privacy. What calls for greater privacy than the decision to have, or not to have, a child? And isn't that decision a case where common sense obtains? (If you don't approve of abortion, don't have one. If you don't want to have a baby, have an abortion.)

Let doctors practice medicine. Let religious zealots practice their religion, but let them keep their religion to themselves. Religious freedom should work two ways: we should be free to practice the religion of our choice, but we must also be free from having someone else's religion practiced on us.

Yet here is the irony in our country today: more than twenty-five years after the *Roe* v. *Wade* decision, the biggest obstacle to safe, legal abortion is not the law—it is the absence of trained abortion providers. (Doctors, again.) The average age of our country's abortion providers is sixty-five.

Throughout the United States, medical students rarely get clinical exposure to abortion. Only 12 percent of OB-GYN residency programs require abortion training. What you hear from many OB-GYN residents is that they're too busy with seriously sick people—they mean in-patient work—to be interested in working at out-patient clinics, where the majority of abortions are provided. (Only 10 percent of abortions are performed in hospitals.) Out-patient clinics were vital in the early days following *Roe* v. *Wade,* but nowadays we might be better off dealing with abortion as a part of family practice. Half the abortions in the United States today could be medical abortions, which means that no surgery would be necessary. (Something the Right-to-Life zealots don't like to be reminded of.)

Many OB-GYN residents don't want to waste their

time with modern-day abortion procedures, which are too simple, too easy to learn. Dr. Judy Tyson, an OB-GYN and abortion provider at Dartmouth-Hitchcock Medical Center, is fond of telling her medical students that she could teach standard surgical-abortion procedure to a chimpanzee in less than an hour. Yet, in more than three quarters of this country's medical schools, standard surgical-abortion procedure is not taught.

The good news is that more and more medical-school students today are turning to family practice. If the OB-GYN community has been reluctant to provide abortion-procedure training, many medical students with an interest in family practice are asking to be trained. Think of women's clinics, Planned Parenthood facilities, and doctors who are known to perform abortions—they have been too easily targeted by the Right-to-Life fanatics. The essential privacy and safety of a woman's right to choose could best be provided by her family doctor.

There is an influential group of young people called Medical Students for Choice. They have over four thousand medical students and residents on their database. Imagine the impact on access to abortion services if even half of these students and residents became abortion providers. Even a quarter would help.

Meanwhile, a self-described Right-to-Lifer approached me in a bookstore where I was signing copies of my ninth

novel, *A Widow for One Year*. She didn't want my auto-
graph. She'd come to the bookstore with her own
agenda—namely, to tell me that I misunderstood the
Right-to-Life movement. "We just want people to be responsible for their children," she told me, giving my hand
a little pat.

I patted her hand right back. I said to her what Dr. Larch
says in *The Cider House Rules:* "If you expect people to be
responsible for their children, you have to give them the
right to choose whether or not to *have* children."

I could see in her eyes that her resolute belief was undi-
minished. She swept out of the bookstore, not pausing to
look at another human face—or at a book.

The young man who stood next in line told me that
she'd cut in front of him; doubtless her zeal to impart her
message was incompatible with the very idea of waiting in
line.

In my opinion, it's not that the decision to have a child
or have an abortion is ever *not* complicated; rather, it is as
morally complex (and often conflicted) a decision as any.
It's never simple. But people who want to *legislate* that
decision—in effect, to make that decision for someone
else—are simply wrong.

# 9 | THE DISINTEGRATING UTERUS

n the novel of *The Cider House Rules,* I transcribed more than one of my grandfather's stories; I gave several of his actual patients to either Homer Wells or Dr. Larch. In the screenplay, I gave Dr. Irving's case of the woman with the disintegrating organs to *both* Homer and Larch.

In real life, my grandfather's patient was a woman hemorrhaging within her abdomen; the name Grandfather gave her was Ellen Bean. Dr. Irving immediately operated and saw that the hemorrhage issued from a six-inch rupture in the back of her uterus. He performed a cesarean section and delivered a stillborn child. But when he tried to sew up Ellen Bean's uterus, his stitches pulled through the tissue, which was the texture of a soft cheese. He had no choice; he had to remove her uterus.

After multiple transfusions, the patient's condition stabilized, but three days later her abdomen again filled with blood. Nor was there any evidence in her strange uterus to explain its disintegrating consistency; even the rupture was a puzzle. There was no scar from a previous cesarean section that could have given way. The placenta could not have weakened the wall of the uterus because the afterbirth had been on the other side of the uterus from the tear. There had been no tumor.

When my grandfather reopened Ellen Bean's wound, there was not as much blood as before, but as he sponged the blood away, he perforated the intestine, and when he lifted up the injured loop to close the hole, his fingers passed as easily through the intestine as through gelatin. His patient was, literally, disintegrating. In three days, she died.

The pathologist told my grandfather that the dead woman had not a trace of vitamin C in her; there was widespread destruction of connective tissue and the tendency to bleed that goes with it. In short, she appeared to have died of scurvy. But Ellen Bean had been a thirty-five-year-old unmarried woman, Dr. Irving knew—not a sailor at sea, deprived of fresh fruits and vegetables.

Then, among the deceased woman's personal effects, Grandfather found what he was looking for. An aborticide called French Lunar Solution. In reality it was oil of tansy, which Ellen Bean had taken for so long, and in such amounts, that her intestines had lost their ability to absorb vitamin C.

In conclusion, my grandfather wrote of this case: "The pregnant state does not engender in all women the rapturous joy traditionally associated with this condition; indeed, there are some who view their future with a sour visage and a jaundiced eye. This much may be assumed from the case of Ellen Bean."

In the novel of *The Cider House Rules,* I gave Ellen Bean's cause of death to the unfortunate Mrs. Eames—"rhymes with screams." (Mrs. Eames is the prostitute from whom Dr. Larch catches the clap.)

In Mrs. Eames's day, oil of tansy wasn't the only aborticide that could kill you. Turpentine was a more common household remedy to an unwanted pregnancy, and women who didn't want babies in the 1880s and '90s were also killing themselves with strychnine and oil of rue.

Since in the screenplay, there wasn't time to develop Larch's history and his relationship-ending relationship with Mrs. Eames, I gave Mrs. Eames's disintegrating uterus to a probable prostitute named Dorothy, and I gave to Homer Wells the correct diagnosis that Dorothy's condition looked like scurvy.

The Dorothy scene, which inspires the aforementioned "lengthiest and most bitter argument" between Larch and Homer on the subject of whether Homer is or isn't a doctor, was edited out of the film. Lasse called me before I'd seen the rough cut. "Don't be angry at me," he said, "but Dorothy is gone." (Lasse was doubtless correct to assume that, in the future editing of the film, a scene dedicated to solving the mystery of a disintegrating uterus was not a surefire keeper.)

In the novel, Dr. Larch performs his first abortion in South Boston on a thirteen-year-old girl. From that moment on, he is a haunted man; the demand to perform more and more abortions follows him like a ghost. In Boston, he wouldn't have lasted long as a hero. ("He detected the dying of conversations upon his entering a room.") That he ends up in an orphanage hospital in the Maine wilderness means that he *can* last as a hero, although Larch doesn't see himself as such. In his voice-over during the film's opening credits, Larch says, "I think I *had* hoped to become a hero, but in St. Cloud's there was no such position." He's wrong, of course. Dr. Larch *creates* the position, not only for himself but for Homer Wells.

In the novel, the description of the condition of Larch's first abortion patient is from my grandfather's description of an extremely small woman he called Edith Fletcher; her pelvis was only three and a half inches in diameter. (A pelvis this small is rare.) And the woman Homer Wells saves from puerperal convulsions was based on an actual patient with the fictitious name of Mrs. Mary O'Toole, a woman my grandfather saved from a similar eclamptic condition in 1937.

Dr. Irving's findings in 1942 were exactly what Dr. Larch and Homer Wells would have found at St. Cloud's in the same year. Syphilis, although a great source of agitation to the public-health officials of the day, afflicted only 2 percent of the pregnant women in Boston. The incidence of eclamptic convulsions was much higher. The disease developed in 8 percent of the country's childbearing women. Thus, in the novel, I felt certain that life in St. Cloud's would not be complete without one good case of eclamptic convulsions, which would surely have tested Homer's skills as a physician. Homer more than passes the test; he makes Larch proud of him.

As for abortion, I consulted a 1928 gynecology textbook by Howard Kelly, the standard work at that time, and assured myself that the term *D and C* would have been in common use when Larch is training Homer.

The vaginal area is prepared with an antiseptic solution. The uterus is examined to estimate its size. One hand is placed on the abdominal wall; two or three fingers of the other hand are in the vagina. A vaginal speculum, which looks like a duck's bill, is inserted in the vagina, allowing the doctor to see the cervix. The cervix is the necklike part of the lower, constricted end of the uterus. The hole in the middle of the cervix is the entrance of the uterus. In pregnancy, the cervix is swollen and shiny.

With a series of metal dilators, the cervix is opened to admit entrance of the ovum forceps. These are tongs with which the doctor grabs at what's inside the uterus. He pulls what he can out. What comes out is called "the products of conception."

With a curette, the wall of the uterus is scraped clean. (The procedure is far simpler today.)

Here is how Homer Wells felt, in the novel, when he performed a D and C on Rose Rose.

. . . he watched the cervix open until it opened wide enough. He chose the curette of the correct size. After the first one, thought Homer Wells, this might get easier. Because he knew now that he couldn't play God in the worst sense; if he could operate on Rose Rose, how could he refuse to help a stranger? How could he refuse anyone? Only a god makes that kind of decision. I'll just give them what they want, he thought. An orphan or an abortion.

Homer Wells breathed slowly and regularly; the steadiness of his hand surprised him. He did not even blink when he felt the curette make contact; he did not divert his eye from witnessing the miracle.

Although he scarcely knew me, I always wanted Grandfather Irving to be proud of me. In the entirety of the novel

*The Cider House Rules,* maybe that passage would have made my grandfather proud. I don't know. Not in the book but in the movie, I tell myself that Grandfather would have appreciated how Homer Wells makes Mr. Rose be "of use" while Homer performs the abortion on Rose Rose. (In the film, Homer makes Mr. Rose hold the ether cone over his daughter's mouth and nose; Mr. Rose also administers the ether, drop by drop.)

You may wonder why it matters to me—namely, what Dr. Irving might have thought of the novel and the film of *The Cider House Rules.* But it is not as a famous physician that I remember my grandfather; it is as a *writer.* Dr. Frederick C. Irving, notwithstanding his considerable medical accomplishments and his overall erudition, loved the lewd and the vulgar. And, one weekend, he gave himself over to an inspired moment of low comedy, in which he expressed that he loved not only the triumphs of obstetrics (over what he called "the relics of barbarism") but that he also loved mankind at its crudest.

If you can't love crudeness, how can you truly love mankind?

With respect to crudeness, here is an interesting point. Some of the audience who will love the movie of *The Cider House Rules* will be readers who didn't love (or even finish) the novel—the principal reason being that they found the novel too crude.

I love Lasse Hallström's film of *The Cider House Rules*, but all of the novel's crude moments are missing from the movie. And don't you suppose that in any story about life in a Maine orphanage earlier in this century, especially a story that focuses on the life of an illegal abortionist's apprentice, there would have been more than a few *very* crude moments? Somebody's disintegrating uterus among them.

n those years when I was writing the novel of *The Cider House Rules* (1981–1985), I was living in New York City—and in a number of rented summer homes in the Hamptons. Concurrently I rented a house in Vermont and another in Massachusetts. I'm not exaggerating when I say that I imagined most of *The Cider House Rules* in my car, a white Saab.

But in 1986 I left New York, and I divested myself of the rented houses in Vermont and Massachusetts. By the time I met Janet, my second wife, I was living full-time in a house I'd bought in Sagaponack.

I must have met Phillip Borsos in New York in 1985, or early in '86, because I already knew him the night I met Janet—she was then my Canadian publisher and she was wearing, unforgettably, a pink dress. (She is now my literary agent, in addition to being my wife.) Phillip was at the dinner party which Janet hosted that night. Phillip and I had already begun working on the screenplay of *The Cider House Rules*. (At the time, I was incapable of even imagining that Phillip would be the first of four directors I would work with on the script—or that the final draft of the screenplay would bear little resemblance to the version he encouraged me to write.)

Coincidentally, Janet and Phillip were friends and had known each other for several years. Coincidences in novels are routinely deplored by book reviewers; yet it has been my observation, from so-called real life, that coincidences abound.

Phillip Borsos was a tall man with long, floppy hair. He spoke gently but persuasively, and his extreme kindness concealed a stubbornness of heroic proportions. I say this in admiration: Phillip may have been the most stubborn man I ever knew. His determination to make a movie of *The Cider House Rules* continued even as he was dying. (Phillip Borsos died of leukemia in 1995; he was forty-two.)

I wrote a dozen or more drafts of the screenplay for Phillip. The first draft was a nine-hour movie. As with any adaptation from a long, plot-driven novel, the problem was what *not* to keep in the film. Even minor characters come with story lines that are interconnected with the main story line. In losing a major minor character, like Melony, I lost part of the main story line, too.

The draft of the *Cider House* screenplay that Phillip and I liked best was the most radical departure from the novel I have written. Since Phillip's death, I have revised that script beyond recognition. The screenplay Lasse Hall-ström and I agreed to shoot, in the fall of 1998, bears a much closer resemblance to the novel than the movie Phillip Borsos and I wanted to make.

The way Phillip and I worked together endeared him to me, but I doubt that my work habits could have endeared me to Phillip. He would gently try to persuade me to do this or that scene a little differently from the way I had written it, or he would gently suggest that I write a scene I had not yet written; sometimes he would gently recom-mend losing an entire character (or two or three).

I would always respond the same way. I'd shout at him. He was pig-headed, he was wrong, he was ruining the story and trivializing the characters—I said this, and worse, routinely. Then I'd go home and think about Phillip's suggestions. To calm myself, I would often watch a video of Phillip's wonderful film *The Grey Fox*.

Eventually I'd sit down and incorporate some of his sug-gestions into the next draft of the screenplay. Naturally we would repeat the process; it worked the same way, every time. Phillip *was* pig-headed, but he was rarely wrong.

While he changed the plot, at times rather recklessly, he never ruined the story—he occasionally made it better—and, far from trivializing the characters, he often made them stronger.

The draft we finally liked was radical for several reasons, all of them involving choices we had made to truncate the story. By eliminating World War II, we eliminated the need for Dr. Larch to invent a heart defect for Homer Wells (to keep Homer out of the war). By eliminating the triangular love story of Homer and Candy and Wally, we eliminated the passage of time; in the movie Phillip and I wanted to make, Homer leaves the orphanage for three months, the duration of only *one* apple harvest, not for fifteen years.

By eliminating Candy and Wally, except as a means for Homer to leave St. Cloud's—he hitches a ride with them after Larch gives Candy an abortion, but he never sees them again after they drive him to the coast—Phillip and I were able to focus on two stories instead of three.

The first story is Homer's life at the orphanage and his conflict with Dr. Larch; the second is Homer's contact with the black migrant apple pickers, and his confrontation with Mr. Rose and his pregnant daughter. Instead of Homer falling in love with Candy, Phillip and I decided to have him fall in love with Rose Rose. (What an awful idea that was.) And eliminating Melony meant that Homer *never* has a love life. (He falls in love with Rose Rose, but she never reciprocates.) Homer returns to St. Cloud's without having had even a brief love affair.

Phillip and I called this "the bleak version." I may have liked it the best—meaning even better than the version that Lasse Hallström shot—but I'll never know. Because of how much I love Lasse's version, I won't speculate further. Phillip died; Lasse got to make the picture his way, not Phillip's.

Suffice it to say that of the four directors who tried to envision the story, Phillip arrived at the grimmest vision. Because I loved Phillip, and was halfway persuaded by him, I felt that Homer without a love life was a deeper and darker character than Homer in love. *The Cider House Rules* was *not* a love story, Phillip Borsos and I decided. It was a history of illegal abortion. The black migrants, Rose Rose and her father, are just other orphans. In a world where that necessary procedure was illegal and unsafe, the *world* was an orphanage. (Hence the cider house, where Homer lives with the apple pickers after he leaves St. Cloud's, and the orphanage of Homer's childhood and young manhood are depressingly similar.)

But in not allowing Homer to have his love story, Phillip and I presented a screenplay for production that was probably too depressing to ever have been made; at least *we* couldn't get it made, although we came close. We held a reading of the script in Paul Newman's living room—Paul was Phillip's first choice to play Dr. Larch, the role ultimately played by Michael Caine—but Paul wasn't convinced.

"There are so many scenes at that incinerator," he said to me, shaking his head. "That incinerator really gets to me."

When Paul turned down the part of Dr. Larch, Phillip and I were discouraged. Without a Larch of Paul Newman's stature, what kind of production money could we attract? The wrong kind, as it turned out. In the world of would-be producers, you can meet some truly vile people, and Phillip and I had the misfortune to meet them.

If serious illness, even cancer, can be caused by stress (as some people maintain), then these particular would-be producers are responsible for Phillip's death. I hold them responsible, anyway. They nearly succeeded in ruining the prospect of *The Cider House Rules* ever being a movie. Nor are they worth mentioning by name or by company; in the landscape of Hollywood, they're as familiar as litter. I think of them as the foam-plastic coffee cups strewn around a construction site, the debris the workers leave behind.

Later, when Phillip got too sick to direct the picture, we tried to find a director to replace him. Ironically, our first choice was Lasse Hallström, the Swedish director who eventually would direct the film—both Phillip and I had loved Hallström's *My Life as a Dog*—but Lasse wasn't available at the time.

When Phillip died, I thought it was unlikely that the movie of *The Cider House Rules* would ever be made. For a while, I didn't think it *should* be made—not without Phillip. All that hardly matters now, because the movie that was made *wasn't* the bleak version.

had tried to write a screenplay only once before I began the script of *The Cider House Rules*. Irvin Kershner wanted to direct a film of *Setting Free the Bears*, my first novel. Kershner had directed *The Luck of Ginger Coffey*, from the Brian Moore novel, and he was (at the time) trying to make a movie of Moore's *The Lonely Passion of Judith Hearne*. I had greatly admired the film of *Ginger Coffey*, and Kershner and I shared a fondness for everything by Brian Moore. In 1969, Columbia Pictures optioned the movie rights to *Setting Free the Bears* and hired me to write the screenplay for Kershner.

I left for Austria in August of that year, buying a red Volvo in Paris en route. The hardcover sales of *Setting Free the Bears* were well below bestseller levels (fewer than ten

thousand copies), but they were better than I'd expected
for a first novel; there'd also been a paperback sale, in addition to the movie option. A Volvo wasn't exactly a luxury
car in those days, but it was *my* first luxury car—meaning
it was the first car I could actually afford. To drive a brand-
new car in Paris, and through France and Switzerland into
Austria . . . well, it's something everyone should do once.
Until that summer, the only other time I'd been in Paris,
I'd been in a bus.

I had not been back to Vienna since I'd been a student
there, at the Institute of European Studies and the Univer-
sity of Vienna, in 1963 and '64. Now, a former professor
of mine, Ernst Winter, rented me a wing of his castle in
the village of Eichbüchl on the outskirts of Wiener
Neustadt—over which my father's squadron had flown,
dropping bombs, more than twenty years before. (My
father, a Slavic languages and literature major at Harvard,
had been a cryptographer for the U.S. Army Air Corps
during World War II.)

*Schloss* Eichbüchl was a real castle, originally built by
Charlemagne. Nazi officers had lived there. Some of them
had been machine-gunned on the stairs leading to the dun-
geon; you could see the pockmarks the bullets had left in
the walls. But in 1969, when I lived at the castle, the dun-
geon was a potato cellar.

The Winter family had uncountable children, most of

whom were teenagers and all of whom were impressive; Kershner and I grew very fond of them while we were writing and rewriting the screenplay for *Setting Free the Bears* in the castle library.

My eldest son, Colin, was four and a half when his brother Brendan was born in Vienna that September. Colin had the run of the castle, which he loved, and the Winter children took turns babysitting for Brendan.

When Kershner and I weren't shouting at each other in the library—Kershner, like me, is a shouter—we were in the war archives in Vienna, watching about forty-eight hours of newsreel footage, most of which detailed Hitler's triumphant arrival in the Austrian capital in 1938. There the *Führer* was, waving from his Mercedes and addressing the multitude in the Heldenplatz (the Plaza of Heroes). Later Hitler spoke to the crowd from a balcony of the Hofburg palace.

There was also some remarkable footage of Göring in *Lederhosen*. He is kissing children at a picnic somewhere near Salzburg. He goes from picnic table to picnic table, grinning ear to ear, kissing the children at every table. The future field marshal was positively charming, and he had such a way with kids that Kershner and I at first failed to recognize him. We kept asking the projectionist, an old man with a patch over one eye, to rewind the film and show us the footage again. The hearty young man kissing the children was very familiar, but we couldn't quite place him.

Finally, in exasperation, Kershner turned to the projectionist. "Who *is* that guy?"

"*Das ist* Hermann Wilhelm Göring," the old man said with great dignity; his one eye, which he turned away from us, was brimming with tears.

While Kershner and I made quick use of the newsreel footage of the *Anschluss,* we could never find a place in the screenplay of *Setting Free the Bears* for Göring to kiss the children at the picnic, although we tried. (I liked the idea of using it during the opening credits.)

It was great fun working with Kershner. He was a wild man with a nonstop imagination and boundless energy. He was also the most passionate reader I ever knew; the man read everything. Kershner was such an enthusiast for the story of *Setting Free the Bears* that he contributed more to the screenplay than I was able to bring to it. He never tired of retelling the story, always in a slightly different way. I just tried to keep up with him, which wasn't easy.

Kershner never sat down. He paced. He would recite the entire story, from the opening shot to the end credits, without once referring to the existent script. I would struggle to write everything down. I felt more like a stenographer than a screenwriter. Kershner was the real screenwriter—I was just taking dictation.

"You changed something! Stop!" I would shout. "You just changed something!"

"Of *course* I changed something!" he would shout back, never stopping or even slowing down. "I'm *always* changing something! It's my *job* to change something!"

Then he would fly back to New York or Los Angeles, leaving me to compose a new script from his notes. It was terribly exciting, but the checks from Columbia Pictures were always late. And there is something about the movie business that is even worse than not being paid—it is the presumption on the part of the people putting up the money that they have an unassailable right to interfere with what happens in the screenplay and with the outcome of the film. (Please don't forget that people put up money to publish books, too. Publishers, among them even the toughest editors, *ask* writers to make changes; they don't tell you that you *have to* make the changes, or simply make them for you.)

Nevertheless, Kershner was my hero, championing each draft of the screenplay, returning to the castle library to shout a new draft into existence.

One spring day we were walking in a pear orchard near *Schloss* Eichbüchl when Kershner paused in midscript to stare at the ground. He had discovered snails.

"Escargot!" he cried.

In Austria they called them *Schnecken,* but they were *es-*

*cargot* to Kershner. We found an empty crate, probably for the pears, and we filled it with the snails. There was a cookbook in the castle that explained how to "purify" snails before cooking them. You put clean lettuce in the crate with them; when they eat the lettuce, they are purified. Somehow.

Frau Winter said that she had purified snails many times, following the instructions in this book. Naturally you had to be sure that the snails were of the edible kind in the first place. Frau Winter assured us that our snails were.

Kershner was very excited to be having escargot. He wanted to bake fresh bread. Did we have enough garlic? he asked.

In the morning, all the snails were dead. Maybe the lettuce had killed them. Maybe they weren't the edible kind, after all, Frau Winter confided to us.

Frau Winter had been one of the Trapp Family Singers—one of the children. She could (and did) tell you some stories. Kershner and I adored her. But Kershner was crestfallen over the death of the snails.

"No escargot," he said. This, together with the late checks, was the earliest sign that the movie of *Setting Free the Bears* was in trouble.

Orson Welles was going to be in it, playing the grandfather. Then Vittorio De Sica was going to be the grandfather. Helmut Berger was going to be Siegfried Javotnik, the doomed hero. Jon Voight was going to be Hannes Graff, the sidekick. Then Al Pacino was going to be Graff. That was how the guys at Columbia Pictures talked (effusively), but their checks came later and later—and, finally, not at all.

I left Vienna for London in May 1970 with my wife and two children, flying home to the United States from London. I'd shipped the Volvo home from France before sailing to England. It arrived in New York weeks later, crusted with salt, the paint faded like that on a forty-year-old car. My Volvo must have crossed the Atlantic on an open deck, or else it was towed behind the ship, making the voyage underwater.

At least the car got there. The same cannot be said for the first couple of chapters of my second novel, *The Water-Method Man,* then in progress. I had shipped the chapters in a steamer trunk, together with some winter clothes, from Vienna to Vermont. The trunk never arrived. I didn't miss the clothes; I rewrote the chapters, probably improving them in the process. From my first experience of writing a screenplay, I had learned something about the process of revision. You can always make something better, and if you make it worse, you'll know it. I had learned to have no fear of rewriting. All writers should be so lucky.

Like most potential movies, *Setting Free the Bears* was never made. But Irvin Kershner has survived unbowed. He is still my hero. I had breakfast with him in Santa Monica about a year and a half ago. We did a lot of wonderful shouting. Kershner hasn't changed in thirty years. Not even directing *The Empire Strikes Back* has aged him—the miraculous "force" is still with him. He was going to direct a film about Puccini, he said. (Actually the main character is a young girl who studies with Puccini, I think.) Once again, Kershner described the story at such a breathtaking pace that I struggled to keep up. Kershner is a passionate enthusiast whose energy is somehow unsullied by the movie business, even though he's in it.

In Santa Monica, the morning sun was beating down on his magnificent bald head. He asked a waiter to move an umbrella in order to shade him from the sun. It was a polite and reasonable request, but Kershner is a movie director in everything he says. There is something commanding even about his politeness. The waiter frantically sought to please him. Soon another waiter and a waitress joined our waiter in the effort to keep Kershner's head in the shade. If it had been cloudy and Kershner had asked for more sun, all of us would have tried to open the heavens for him.

Naturally Kershner and I remembered aloud the considerable energy we had expended on behalf of *Setting Free the Bears* at *Schloss* Eichbüchl. We also talked about Frau Winter, the former Trapp singer, who is dead now, and her wonderful children, who once looked after Brendan. Kershner was shocked at the news of Frau Winter's death; to him, she seemed indestructible. On his face was the genuine outrage and sorrow that I saw there when the snails died, and when Columbia Pictures pulled the plug on *Setting Free the Bears*.

The next movie director to enter my life was George Roy Hill, who directed *The World According to Garp.* There was never any danger of the plug being pulled on George. He was an ex-Marine; he took charge of everyone. The success of *Butch Cassidy and the Sundance Kid* and *The Sting* had made the team performances of Paul Newman and Robert Redford renowned, and George had been their general. He commanded a loyal following of people who'd worked with him before—among them Bobby Crawford, his producer, and Marion Dougherty, his old friend and casting director.

On one of the *Garp* locations, in Millbrook, New York—the site of the so-called Steering Academy—two distinguished guests visited the set, Paul Newman one day, James Cagney another. At the time I wondered why such veteran actors would come to a movie set in the summer heat to watch a small, unmemorable scene be shot over and over again—for two or three hours. Later I understood why. They were not only paying their respects to George; they wanted to watch the general with his troops.

Even in the smallest scene, to see George *in control* was inspiring. He was the epitome of the commanding officer you would willingly die for; he conveyed the kind of courage that convinced you he would unhesitatingly die for you, too. Handsome, courtly, and with a bad back— from crashing a plane, I was told—George was also a pilot. He was one of those men you put your trust in absolutely.

Yet when George asked me to write the screenplay for *Garp,* I declined. I was writing my fifth novel, *The Hotel New Hampshire,* at the time; I knew very little about the movie business, but I knew enough not to stop a novel to start a screenplay.

"I'll ask you only once," George told me. He was true to his word. Steve Tesich wrote the script for *Garp.*

When George showed me Steve's first draft, I didn't like it. Now it's easy to see that I have been much more extreme in translating two of my novels into screenplays— *The Cider House Rules* and *A Son of the Circus*—than Steve Tesich was with *Garp.* But at the time I believed that the best adaptation from a novel to a film was a literal one.

We are always more permissive of our own extremism

than we are of someone else's. Steve changed Vienna to
New York—that took some getting used to. And there is an
airplane that crashes into Garp's house just before he buys
the house, thus (in Garp's mind) making the house safe
from other disasters. (Naturally, he's wrong.) There is no
airplane in the novel. In the film, George Roy Hill himself
plays the pilot who walks away from the crash, unharmed.
In the end, as Garp is dying, a helicopter carries him away.

"*What* helicopter?" I asked George.

But these details are more *Garp*-like than I first thought;
in the movie, they work. A more enduring problem is the
difference between Steve Tesich's sense of humor and
mine. Steve was a guy who told jokes—good ones, but
jokes. Like many comics, he had a gift for one-liners. The
first draft of the screenplay was riddled with wisecracks.

I don't do one-liners. What's comic in my novels is not
what my characters *say;* my comedy is not the comedy of
quips. The whole situation is comic; the entire reaction of
the characters to their situation is what's funny, if anything is.

In subsequent drafts, Steve laid off the one-liners, but a
few survived; they still make me wince whenever I see the
film, although for the most part, George (as he said he
would) directed over them. He instructed the actors to
soften those lines that appeared to me to jump off the
page.

The principal success of the film of *The World According to Garp* should be credited to Marion Dougherty's good instincts for casting and how George directed the actors. I thought that all the characters, minor to major, were perfect. What was missing from the movie was chiefly mitigated by the performances of the actors.

George was right to have faith in Robin Williams; Robin was an excellent Garp. His only noticeable discomfort with the role was that he had too much body hair to convincingly play Garp as a teenager; hence, for those scenes, he was waxed. The sounds of Robin screaming from the trailer, where he was being waxed in preparation for the blow-job scene, are memorable to this day.

My eldest son, Colin, was assigned the task of coaching Robin to wrestle. Robin was a good athlete, and he took to the daily workouts with unbridled zeal. Maybe too much zeal; Colin's chief concern was that Robin might get hurt. George was very stern with Colin on the subject of not breaking Robin's arms or giving him a mat burn on his forehead, but Robin remained injury-free and unmarked throughout the filming.

When I first met Glenn Close, who played Jenny Fields, Garp's mother, I thought she was far too young and sexy for the role—Jenny's sexual abstemiousness is essential to her radicalism. Yet, with or without her starched nurse's uniform, Glenn's militantly upper-class voice made her a believably sexless Jenny. Mary Beth Hurt was also perfect, as Garp's wife, Helen, and John Lithgow (as the transsexual Roberta Muldoon) was magnificent. Even the minor parts were matchless—Swoosie Kurtz as the prostitute, whom Garp's mother buys for him, and Amanda Plummer as the tongueless rape victim, Ellen James.

It was a movie experience that spoiled me because I was able to remain detached from it. It was not my screenplay and no longer my novel; it was a George Roy Hill film, and I liked George Roy Hill films. I was very well treated, but—at the same time—I was never truly involved. That I accepted a cameo role as the referee of a wrestling match was an accident; I just happened to be on the set when the scene came up. I'd been certified as a referee for twenty-four years; it wasn't as if I was called upon to act. As it turned out, I did have to remember a couple of lines, which I found difficult to say; they were Steve Tesich's lines, not mine.

Now Steve is dead, and George has Parkinson's disease; it's sad to think we'll never see a new George Roy Hill film. I still get together with Robin Williams and John Lithgow, but only occasionally; we exchange Christmas cards, silently observing (with the shock of all families) how our children have grown.

Most of the others from the *Garp* film have slipped away. Sometimes, looking through my address book, I come upon a phone number that I haven't called in years. It may not still be a working number; I'm tempted to call, just to see. But I never make the call. I never cross out the name and number, either.

A film is a fast family, almost an instant family. It is also quickly over. In the working life of a novel, the supporting cast is relatively small—my wife (my first reader), a friend or two, my editor. Occasionally, depending on the degree of research necessary for the novel, there are a few "expert" readers—doctors for a novel about a doctor, for example. These relationships generally endure beyond the writing of the particular book; something remains. But with a movie, there is this sudden, intense grouping of a lot of people, many of whom will never see one another again.

Then one night, on the television, I am searching for a film or a ball game, and there are Glenn Close and Robin Williams—the unlikely mother with her unlikely son. Seeing them is *not* like taking one of my books down from the shelf and encountering a specific and familiar passage. Glenn and Robin may be familiar in the predictability of their behavior, but they are also strangers, merely wearing the clothes I gave them, which they are only borrowing for a while. One has seen them wear other clothes.

George Roy Hill also directed the film of *Slaughterhouse-Five,* from the Kurt Vonnegut novel. Kurt was my teacher at Iowa, and an old friend. We went to see an early screening of *Garp* together. Before the screening, Kurt warned me: "It's like seeing your characters get their hair cut." (And they're prettier, they smell better, they don't swear as much. I suppose they're more presentable to the rest of the world.)

In the case of *Garp,* George followed a clean narrative line through the domestic story of the novel, which was the story of a mother and her son, and of the son's marriage. What George left out was what Vonnegut called "the rough stuff"—the more unseemly, more sordid parts of the story.

What Kurt said wasn't offered as criticism; it was just an observation, and I think it's true. (Well, okay, maybe you liked them a *little* better when their hair was long and shaggy.)

# 13 | THE MOTORCYCLE
# I GAVE AWAY

Then there was Tony Richardson, the nonpareil. I've never felt as flattered as when Tony told me he wanted to make a movie of *The Hotel New Hampshire*, my fifth novel. I loved Tony Richardson's films. He had a range like no one else—violent or austere one minute, wildly comic the next. *The Loneliness of the Long Distance Runner* and *The Loved One, Tom Jones* and *The Border*. I had no doubt what Tony Richardson would do with *The Hotel New Hampshire*—a macabre comedy and a fairy tale, not half as realistic as *Garp*. Tony didn't even pretend to be disappointed when I told him I didn't want to write the screenplay; he wanted to write it himself, which he did.

It was a brilliant screenplay, but Tony's original vision of

*The Hotel New Hampshire* was of a film in two parts. Some critics of the novel had recoiled at the degree of sexual farce. Not Tony. The film couldn't be sexual or farcical enough to satisfy him. His was an uncompromising vision. He would leave nothing out; he would capture the *whole* novel, he said.

But now that I've had more experience in the movie business, I accept that most films are exercises in compromise. Tony was unprepared to compromise. When Orion Pictures insisted on making one movie, not a film in two parts, Tony refused to significantly cut the script; he shortened scenes, he used a lot of montage, he increased the voice-over, which fastforwarded many scenes, but in essence he deleted not a single story line or minor character from his two-movie screenplay. The rousing choice of music (Jacques Offenbach) gave to the film the lunatic, exuberant pace of the cancan.

Many good films, like *Garp,* are toned-down versions of the books they come from; Tony Richardson's *The Hotel New Hampshire* is a deliberate exaggeration of the novel. By speeding up the story to the Offenbach score, Tony heightened both the comedic and the fairy-tale qualities of the book; he enhanced the hectic narrative momentum of the novel. But he paid a price. Many of the minor (and even the major minor) characters were reduced to caricatures—they became cartoon versions of themselves. (Another oft-heard criticism of the film is that you need to have read the novel to know who many of the characters are. Knowing the novel as well as I do, I can't speak to that charge.)

In addition to fastforwarding many scenes, the voice-over imitated the novel's persistent foreshadowing accurately, but many film critics have a knee-jerk objection to voice-over, and both film and book reviewers are often suspicious of flashforwarding. (Note: this is not a typographical error. *Fast*forwarding and *flash*forwarding are two different things.) In the narrative voice of a novel, or in voice-over, what I mean by "flashforwarding" is any voice of authority that does this kind of thing: "Ten years later, I would regret running over Mrs. Abernathy's cocker spaniel, but at the time it seemed that the episode would quickly pass."

In a recent review of *A Widow for One Year,* a book reviewer went so far as to say that the flashforward has a "lesser ontological status" than the flashback; furthermore, the reviewer concluded, the flashforward is "a subversive, supernatural process." You bet it is. If a novelist or a movie director can't play God, who can?

Whether in the narrative voice of a novel *or* in voice-over, what the flashforward does is invite the audience to have a look at the storytelling mechanism itself. Rather than label that process "subversive" or "supernatural," I would contend that most readers and moviegoers *like* to be given hints of the future. One of the pleasures provided by storytelling, in both a novel and a film, is anticipation.

In the film of *The Hotel New Hampshire*, Tony Richardson made a purposeful choice—heighten the farce. He fastforwarded *and* flashforwarded like crazy. In the novel, John Berry (Rob Lowe in the film) is in love with his older sister, Franny (Jodie Foster); John's infatuation with Franny is both agonizing and bittersweet. In the movie, Tony chose to make John Berry's incestuous obsession with his sister a comic romp. As for Franny, a rape victim who is later seduced by a terrorist, Tony gave her a tomboy's enduring toughness and a kind of in-your-face sexual swagger.

But John's infatuation with Franny was hard for me to *see*. In the film, I could never convince myself that Rob Lowe, a gorgeous boy—prettier than most girls—could be head over heels for Jodie Foster. Ms. Foster was not nearly as attractive as a young girl as she has become; she is a good-looking young woman, and a terrific actress, but she was *not* a pretty girl. In the movie, I could have been more easily convinced that Jodie Foster was obsessed with Rob Lowe.

That said, if the incest wasn't convincing, Jodie Foster and Rob Lowe were otherwise right for their roles, and their supporting cast was first-rate. Beau Bridges as the heedlessly dreaming father was superb; he was exactly as I'd imagined the father of that unfortunate family. And Tony's decision to make Franny's rapist and her terrorist-seducer the same actor (Matthew Modine) was shrewd. Mr. Modine was especially good as the terrorist without a conscience, as was Amanda Plummer in her role as the terrorist *with* a conscience. (Ms. Plummer, who is tongueless in *Garp,* is also handicapped in *The Hotel New Hampshire,* where her nickname is "Miss Miscarriage.")

The more eccentric characters, Iowa Bob (Wilford Brimley) and Freud (Wallace Shawn), suffered less as caricatures than did some relatively more realistic minor characters, and both Brimley and Shawn were wonderful. Somewhat less successful in the film was the tragicomic character of Susie the bear (Nastassja Kinski). It was not Ms. Kinski's fault, although her being visibly pregnant during the shooting did not help her cause. Perhaps she'd mistakenly assumed that she would be wearing the bear suit in all her scenes—hence no one would know she was pregnant. But, alas, there was an all-important love scene between her and Rob Lowe, when of course she was out of her ursine costume—and any other costume—and which Tony was forced to shoot in the half-dark. It was a shame not to see more of her, I thought.

It was Susie who suffered most from the cartoon effects

on the characters; she was the principal victim of Tony speeding up two movies to turn them into one. Only once, when Ms. Kinski is dirty-haired and shambling through the Prater in her bear suit (without the head, which she is toting like a lunch pail in one paw), does Susie the bear look like the sexually wounded character she is. She is a symbol for all the sexually wounded, which is what *The Hotel New Hampshire* is about.

I liked the movie nonetheless. Tony's interpretation of the novel as sexual cancan is a much more suitable translation of my sense of humor than Steve Tesich's dialogue in *The World According to Garp.* But, to most audiences, *The Hotel New Hampshire* was not nearly as successful a film as *Garp.* Only in some countries in Europe was it more popular, which may have been the result of *Hotel* being more popular in parts of Europe as a book, too—I mean more popular than *Garp.* (The film's success in Europe may also have been the result of Tony Richardson and Nastassja Kinski being better known there than they are in North America. I don't know.)

Earlier, before Orion Pictures was involved, there had been some effort to finance the film of *The Hotel New Hampshire* with money from an interested pizza billionaire. "The pizza money," Tony called it. But soon the pizza magnate began to behave like a producer. "Even the pizza man has an opinion!" Tony said.

Somewhere along the line, the pizza man's money was spurned and Orion Pictures became the major player; maybe that was when Tony's idea of a film in two parts was compromised. Tony's old friend, and *The Hotel New Hampshire*'s producer, Neil Hartley, tried to explain the intricacies of film financing to me once, but I have never been able to grasp it. Neil was very kind and patient with me, but he might as well have been describing the pleasures and perils of hang gliding to a mole.

Tony Richardson died of AIDS in November 1991. His memoir, *The Long-Distance Runner,* was found by his daughter Natasha on the day of his death; Tony had hidden it in the back of the same cupboard where he kept his Oscars. I miss him. Like Irvin Kershner, Tony was a great reader and a good friend. He was not just another eccentric Englishman living in Los Angeles; he lived there like deposed but flamboyant royalty, like a king who relished his own exile.

There is a picture that was taken of us on one of the locations for *The Hotel New Hampshire,* an abandoned school somewhere in Quebec. It's raining. Tony's poncho balloons around him like a sail. I'm standing in the archway of the massive door to the old school. Tony, standing a step down from me, is still half a head taller than I am. He is standing defiantly in the rain, in profile, his distinctive nose like the beak of an inquisitive bird of prey. For no reason that I can remember, Tony is wearing black elbow-length gloves—like the fireproof, heat-resistant gloves of a man who works in a forge. He wore his eccentricity like that—baffling and absurd, but also with the appearance of something casually acquired, to which he was indifferent. (God knows what those gloves meant to Tony—probably nothing.) That he struck others as bizarre did not matter to him.

I was teaching at the Bread Loaf Writers' Conference in Ripton, Vermont, when Tony finished shooting the motor-cycle scenes in *The Hotel New Hampshire*. To find a vintage motorcycle with a sidecar had not been difficult; a larger problem had been to make the sidecar strong enough to carry the bear. (I mean a *real* bear, not Nastassja Kinski.) In both the novel and the film, Freud drives the bear named State o' Maine around in the sidecar. Wally Shawn must have loved that.

To my surprise, Tony sent me the motorcycle. There was still bear hair in the sidecar. The motorcycle and side-car had been boxed up and trucked from Quebec to Ver-mont. It was an illegal, unlicensed vehicle, and dangerous because its brakes were only equipped to stop a motorcy-cle less than half its power and size. On the dirt roads around Bread Loaf, my son Colin's preferred method of stopping the machine was to drive off the road and wedge the sidecar between two trees—with my son Brendan in the sidecar. As the father (at the time) of two teenage boys, I quickly decided what to do with the motorcycle; I gave it away.

"Pity," Tony told me later. "If I'd been able to arrange it, I would have sent you the bear."

# 14 | NOT COMPLETELY HEALED

n early 1989, when my seventh novel, *A Prayer for Owen Meany,* was about to be published, I was at loose ends. My screenplay of *The Cider House Rules* was in its fourth year of not going into production, and I was a recently retired wrestling coach who was between novels. I don't like being "between novels," especially when a new novel is being published and I haven't the next novel firmly in mind. (What would turn out to be my eighth novel, *A Son of the Circus,* was a long way from being "firmly in mind.")

My son Brendan had just won the New England Class A title at 135 pounds, and I had happily retired from coaching wrestling—again. I had first retired in 1983, when my son Colin won the New England Class A title at 160 pounds. But this time I was forty-seven; I knew I had coached (and had retired from coaching) for the last time.

Sometime that spring, when *A Prayer for Owen Meany* was solidly holding the number-two position on the *New York Times* bestseller list, I talked to Salman Rushdie on the phone. (We'd met in London ten years earlier and had been friends ever since.) Following the death threat against him (in February 1989), Salman had gone underground; he was somewhere in England, I presumed, when he called. The number-one bestseller on the *New York Times* list that spring was *The Satanic Verses,* the book responsible for the *fatwa* against Salman.

I made a mock complaint to him . . . something along the lines that *Owen Meany* would surely have made the number-one spot on the *Times* list if I hadn't had the misfortune to be published at exactly the same time as his *Satanic Verses.*

"You want to trade places?" he asked.

No. I did not. We talked for a while about the next novel I thought I wanted to write. "It's about an Indian-born doctor living in Toronto," I told Salman. "He's a Canadian citizen, but he doesn't feel assimilated into Canadian culture—he doesn't feel very Canadian. And when he goes back to India, which he does periodically, he doesn't feel like an Indian, either. He's a foreigner both in his country of birth and where he lives."

"So what's different, or at least interesting, about him?" Salman asked.

That was the problem, I admitted. I was working on it; that was all I could say.

Something about orthopedic surgery seemed to me to be the key. Could it have to do with the difference between the kind of patients an orthopedic surgeon sees in Toronto as opposed to Bombay? There are more crippled children in India. Then I read an article in a medical journal on the subject of the most common form of short-limbed dwarfism, achondroplasia, for which (at the time) a genetic marker had not been found. Maybe my doctor was an amateur geneticist, taking blood from achondroplastic dwarfs? *That* might be a little different, or at least a little interesting.

That's as far as I was with *A Son of the Circus,* which I would end up dedicating to Salman, when the photographer Mary Ellen Mark and her husband, Martin Bell, a British filmmaker, came to visit me in my house in Sagaponack. (Martin has since become an American citizen; he directed *American Heart.*)

Mary Ellen and Martin were old friends of mine, but we'd never worked together. That weekend they brought some new photographs of Mary Ellen's to show me. She had spent a lot of time photographing the small circuses of India, principally the child performers in those circuses.

And there suddenly, in the photographs, were my doctor's dwarfs—achondroplastic dwarfs, the clowns of the Indian circus. My doctor could make a study of them; he could draw their blood, I thought.

This led to a further thought about my doctor: of more interest to me than his profession, which was orthopedic surgery, was his passionate *amateur* pursuit—the dwarfs' blood, the search for the as-yet-unidentified gene for achondroplasia. But what might the doctor's *other* hobbies be? I'd known many doctors who wanted to be writers, or who fancied themselves as writers already. Why not make my doctor a screenwriter? Of course I knew he would be a bad one, just as I knew he would never find the genetic marker for achondroplasia. (So much for hobbies.)

Something magical happened later. Almost simultaneously with the publication of *A Son of the Circus,* a doctor in California found the gene for achondroplastic dwarfism. In a letter, he admitted to me that he'd found the genetic marker for achondroplasia without having met a single dwarf.

But at the end of the summer of 1989, Martin Bell and I knew only that we had a story (or parallel stories) in common. Martin wanted to make a documentary film about the child performers in an Indian circus—probably about one child performer in particular, he said. Would a feature film on that subject interest me? Martin asked. Did

I want to write a screenplay about the fate of a child (or children) sold to an Indian circus? We could go to India and research the story together.

That fall, I wrote the first draft of a screenplay—at the time titled *Escaping Maharashtra*. I also took some notes for my novel about an Indian-born doctor and his dwarf-blood research, and his work with crippled children in Bombay. The doctor is passionate about circuses because of the dwarfs, but he also knows that many of the performers are children who've been sold to the circus by their parents. (The parents know that their children will have a better life in the circus.) The doctor, in addition to his dwarf research and his screenwriting, develops another amateur pursuit—rescuing street children from Bombay and placing them in Indian circuses.

Naturally the circuses will take only the most talented acrobats and street performers among these abandoned children. Mary Ellen told me that the girls might otherwise become child prostitutes. The majority of the child performers in the Indian circuses are girls. But what if one of these gifted girls had a crippled brother? What could a crippled child do in the circus?

That became the link between my orthopedic surgeon, with an interest in dwarf blood and crippled children, and the circus.

I went to India in January 1990, by which time the par-

**John Irving as the disapproving stationmaster.**

*(All photographs: Stephen Vaughan / ©Miramax Films)*

The director Lasse Hallström directing John Irving,
the disapproving stationmaster, on the set of *The Cider House Rules*
in Bellows Falls, Vermont.

The producer Richard Gladstein with the disapproving stationmaster.

A younger Dr. Wilbur Larch (Michael Caine) and Nurse Angela
(Kathy Baker) and Nurse Edna (Jane Alexander) watch
Homer Wells leave the orphanage for Homer's second adoption;
they know he'll be back.

Homer Wells
(Tobey Maguire),
the unadoptable
orphan.

Dr. Larch (Michael Caine), the orphanage physician—obstetrician, gynecologist, abortionist.

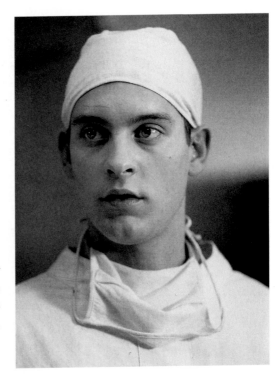

Homer— physician-in-training, the abortionist's apprentice.

Larch and Homer, naming the babies.

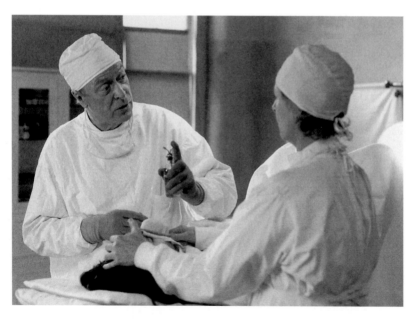

Diagnosing Dorothy's disintegrating uterus. The Dorothy
scene was cut from the film.

Lasse directing the children in the dining hall at St. Cloud's. Spencer Diamond is Curly.

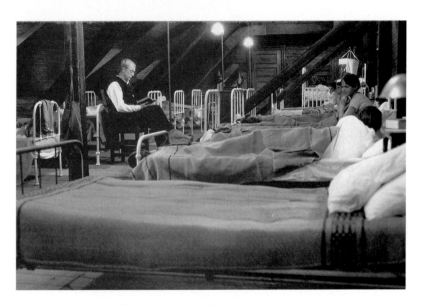

Larch reading Dickens to the boys in the bunk room.

Nurse Edna (Jane Alexander) in the girls' bunk room.

Buster (Kieran Culkin).

Homer carrying the operating-room pail to the
incinerator, Buster following.

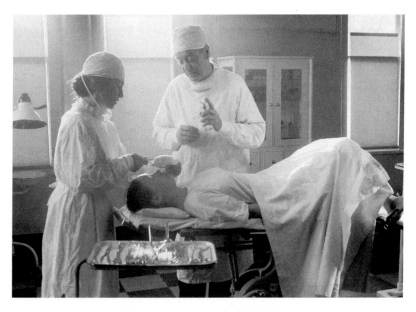

Nurse Angela (Kathy Baker) holds the ether cone,
Dr. Larch the ether bottle.

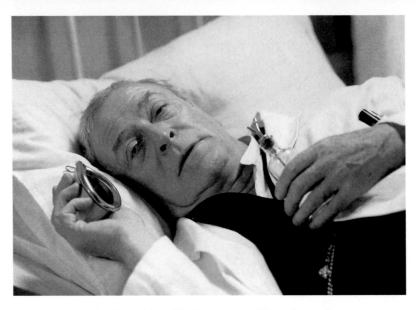

Larch giving himself ether. An accidental overdose
will eventually kill him.

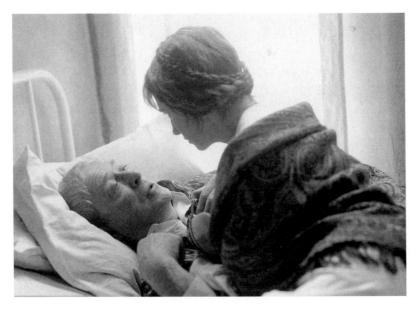

Nurse Angela wakes Larch from an ether sleep.

**Mary Agnes (Paz de la Huerta).**

**Nurse Edna discovers the twelve-year-old girl by the incinerator.**

The twelve-year-old girl (Kasey Berry). She dies of a botched abortion; she comes to St. Cloud's too late for Larch to save her.

Lasse directing Michael, Tobey, and Jane in the operating room with the twelve-year-old girl.

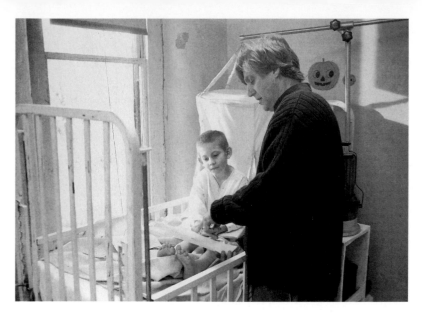

**Lasse directing Erik Sullivan as Fuzzy.**

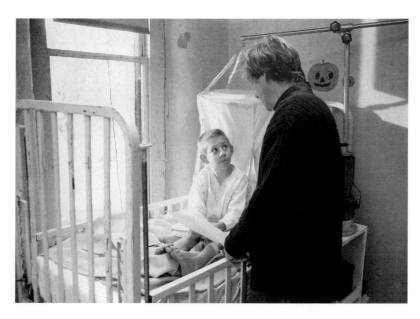

**Michael Caine called Erik a "treasure"—a gift to the film.**

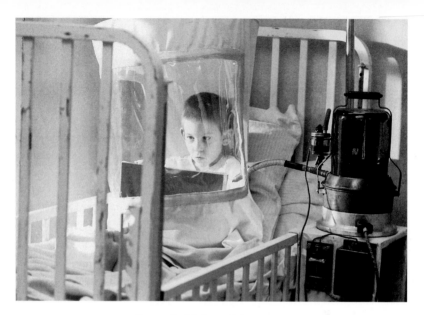

Fuzzy in his breathing tent.

Lasse with Charlize Theron (Candy) and Paul Rudd (Wally).

When Candy arrives at the orphanage in St. Cloud's, the orphans swarm around her and Wally's car.

Candy being interviewed in Larch's office, before her abortion. ("How many months are you?" Homer asks her.)

**Fuzzy watching Homer Wells leave St. Cloud's.**

The producer (Richard Gladstein) and the screenwriter
(John Irving) on the set of the apple orchards and the cider house
in Dummerston, Vermont.

Wally brings Homer to the cider house for the first time.

Mr. Rose (Delroy Lindo) with his daughter, Rose Rose (Erykah Badu).

Rose Rose. ("I know when someone is in trouble,
Homer, and you is.")

Muddy (K. Todd Freeman). ("This here sensitive-lookin' fella," Mr. Rose calls him.)

Peaches (Heavy D) and Hero (Lonnie R. Farmer) laugh when Homer reads the first of the cider house rules: "Don't smoke in bed."

Wally driving Homer through the orchards. ("Close your eyes," Wally tells him. "This is flying on instrument.")

Homer Wells, apple
picker.

Mr. Rose: "You don't wanna go into the knife business with me."
Jack (Evan Dexter Parke) is in the foreground of the scene.

After the knife fight—Mr. Rose has won the fight but he cut himself in the process—Rose Rose stitches up her father's hand. Homer is critical of her method. ("I s'pose you is a doctor, Homer," Rose Rose says. "Almost," he tells her.)

The end of the first harvest; the pickers are leaving in their truck, on the road again.

Lasse on the beach in Maine, preparing the love scene
between Homer and Candy.

Homer and Candy on the beach.

Candy with Homer in the cider house. Wally's away at the war,
and the pickers are gone; apples are not in season.

Candy is hiding.
Olive (Wally's mother)
has just brought Homer
some extra blankets
for the winter.

Candy is getting dressed in a hurry. She and Homer have heard Mr.
Rose's truck; the pickers have returned for the second harvest.

Larch showing Fuzzy *King Kong*, a private screening. The film breaks—
Larch calls it "Homer's splice"—and Fuzzy dies.

Larch and Buster bury Fuzzy. ("We'll tell the little ones
he was adopted," Larch says to Buster. Buster questions why the
little ones will believe it. "They'll believe it because they
*want* to believe it," Larch replies.)

Edna and Angela with Dr. Larch in his office. Larch has falsified a
college and a medical-school degree for Homer Wells.
Angela complains that Homer's credentials are against the law.
"Don't you be holy to me about the law," Larch tells her. "What has
the law done for any of us here?"

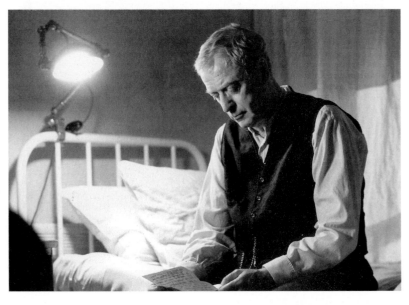

Larch reads Homer's letter; Homer says he's not
coming back to St. Cloud's. ("I fear we've lost him to the world,"
Larch will tell Angela.)

Major Winslow (Colin Irving) delivers the news about Wally to Wally's mother, and to Candy and Homer. Wally has been shot down over Burma; he has encephalitis B. ("Captain Worthington is paralyzed . . . from the waist down. He won't walk again.")

Homer and Candy on the dock by the lobster pens, after hearing the news about Wally. Homer has told Candy that Wally can still produce children; he can have "a normal sex life." Homer also tells her that he'll do whatever she wants, but Candy says she wants to do "nothing."

Lasse directing Tobey before the abortion scene in the cider house.

Homer prepares his surgical instruments before performing the abortion on Rose Rose.

After his daughter's abortion, Mr. Rose confronts Homer over the cider
house rules; the rules are tacked onto the beam between them.
("Them rules ain't for *us*," Mr. Rose tells Homer. "We makin' our *own*
rules, every day. Ain't that right, Homer?")

Dr. Larch's burial; Larch is buried in the graveyard at St. Cloud's,
beside Fuzzy and the twelve-year-old girl.

**Homer Wells comes home to St. Cloud's.**

**Lasse directing Tobey on how to read the passage
from *David Copperfield* to the boys.**

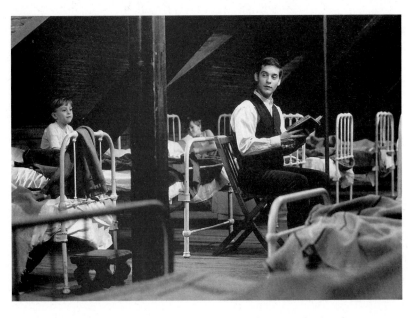

**Homer, like Larch, reading Dickens to the boys in the bunk room.**

allel stories of my screenplay and my novel were increasingly connected. The novel was already called *A Son of the Circus.* Not long after Martin Bell and I returned from India, my screenplay, *Escaping Maharashtra,* was retitled, becoming *A Son of the Circus,* too. Thus this screenplay was never an adaptation of the novel (like *The Cider House Rules*). In fact, the screenplay was finished—except for fine-tuning—several years before I finished the novel. With any luck, Martin and I might have seen the film produced, and even released, before the novel was published. But that kind of luck we didn't have.

Martin was also unlucky in another respect. In Junagadh, at the Great Royal Circus, he was bitten in the face by a rabid chimpanzee. I was in Bombay at the time; the call came that I was to carry the rabies vaccine in a thermos. But keeping the vaccine cool all the way to Junagadh was impossible. The plane from Bombay to Rajkot was delayed. Ramu, the driver from the circus who met us at the airport in a battered Land Rover, required another couple of hours to navigate the road between Rajkot and Junagadh.

In the novel, I described that trip in the Land Rover as follows: "The landscape of hideously slain animals flew by . . . [we] hurtled through the darkened countryside and the dimly lit towns, where the reek of cooking and excrement assailed [us]—together with the squabbling of chickens, the barking of dogs and the savage threats of the shouting, almost-runover pedestrians. Ramu apologized that his driver's-side window was missing; not only did the rushing night air grow cooler, but the back-seat passengers were struck by flying insects."

In Junagadh, "the streets were teeming; two crowds were surging against each other. A loudspeaker on a parked truck played circus music. One crowd was coming from the early-evening show, the other hurrying to line up for the show that was to start later on. . . . Although Ramu never stopped blowing his horn, the Land Rover barely crawled through the crowd. Several small boys clung to the door handles and the rear bumper, allowing themselves to be dragged along the road. . . . Far ahead of them, a dwarf clown on stilts was leading the throng. It was even more congested at the circus because it was too early to let the crowd in; the Land Rover had to inch its way through the well-guarded gate."

The rabies vaccine in the thermos was tepid by the time I delivered it to Martin, but the stuff worked. In addition to the bites on Martin's face and neck, a clump of his beard was gone and he'd been bitten on one hand (while trying to keep the chimpanzee from biting his throat). It had been a 160-pound chimp that had jumped on Martin from the back of a horse. A great way to begin our research at the circus.

In Bombay, I'd visited a children's hospital, a private club, a police station, a library, and the brothels on Falkland Road, but the time I spent with Martin and Mary Ellen at the Great Royal Circus in Junagadh—most of the month of January—was the really important time. That was when the parallel but separate stories of the screenplay and the novel clearly emerged.

The screenplay would be the story of what Dr. Daruwalla *wished* had happened to the children in the circus and to the Jesuit missionary. The crippled boy learns how to perform the skywalk. (In the novel, he falls and dies.) His beautiful sister is killed instantly by a lion. (In the novel, she runs away from the circus to become a child prostitute in Bombay, where she dies of AIDS.) And the Jesuit missionary gives up his vows; he falls in love with a woman in the circus—a former trapeze artist, now training the children. (In the novel, the missionary also gives up his vows, but he's a homosexual; he doesn't fall in love with a woman.)

Yet the essential characters and the atmosphere for both the screenplay and the novel were the same. In the novel, Dr. Daruwalla (the screenwriter) creates a scapegoat to portray himself; embarrassed at his amateurism, his failure to find the genetic marker for achondroplasia, Dr. Daruwalla invents a young American doctor and makes *him* the idealistic fool who's obsessed with getting the dwarfs' blood. (In the screenplay, Dr. Daruwalla is a minor character, but a dignified one; dwarf research would be beneath him.)

That winter I was in Junagadh, the leader of the dwarf clowns was named Shivaji. I had already studied achondroplasia; I knew that an achondroplastic dwarf could be born of normal parents, and that the dwarf's children would have a 50 percent chance of being dwarfs. This type of dwarfism is most often the result of a rare genetic event, a spontaneous mutation, which then becomes a dominant characteristic in the dwarf's children.

Shivaji's parents had been normal. Shivaji's only child was a dwarf. Shivaji's wife was normal, and—to use his own description of her—"almost beautiful." But she'd come from a very poor family; she had no dowry. "Only a dwarf would marry her," Shivaji explained.

Sitting in his tent, I was unsuccessful in convincing Shivaji that his existence was probably the result of "a rare genetic event, a spontaneous mutation"; he didn't believe in genes, he told me.

Shivaji was no less suspicious of my fictional doctor. "What does this guy want with our blood?" he asked.

I explained that my doctor was looking for the secret thing that made him a dwarf.

"It's no secret," Shivaji told me. He thought he knew all about it. He said he was a dwarf because, on the morning his mother conceived, she looked out the window and the first living thing she saw was a dwarf. "That did it," Shivaji explained.

What about his son, who was also a dwarf? That was because, on the morning his wife conceived, she rolled over and looked at Shivaji. "I told her not to look at me, but she did," he said. "Your doctor is wasting his time," Shivaji added.

I tried again. "My doctor is looking for something in the dwarfs' blood, which—if he finds it—will help other people not to give birth to dwarfs."

"Why should I help your doctor put an end to dwarfs?" Shivaji asked. An unanswerable question.

In the novel, I gave Shivaji's firmly held opinions to the character Vinod. In the screenplay, I let Shivaji be Shivaji— I hoped that he might get a chance to play himself. That wasn't to be. (I presume that my Shivaji is still a clown in the Great Royal Circus, but we will use a different circus in the film.)

Although it took me five and a half years to write the novel of *A Son of the Circus,* once I finished, the book was published on schedule in 1994. The screenplay was first scheduled to go into production in the fall of 1997, but that fell through. The film was then scheduled for production in the winter of 1999. Jeff Bridges was cast as the missionary both times. And, both times, the film came up short by exactly the same amount of money: $1.5 million. Thus the second production fell through as well.

This is a notable difference between a novel and a film. A novel that has been accepted for publication, and has been edited for publication—and is in all other respects *ready* for publication—does not "fall through." That is one of the principal reasons I prefer my day job as a novelist to my occasional job as a screenwriter. I can count on the fingers of one hand the number of truly good novels I have read in manuscript that have *not* been published, but good screenplays don't get made into movies all the time. (More's the pity—so many bad ones *do*.)

As of this writing, Martin Bell isn't leaving for India anytime soon. It's been nine years since we were in Junagadh together. Martin's face is completely healed. But not really.

In the novel of *A Son of the Circus,* I made comic use of that chimp attack—a "racist chimpanzee," upon spotting the unfamiliarly fair-skinned missionary among a sea of all-brown faces, bites off the missionary's earlobe. After the biting, the missing earlobe cannot be found.

Of course I know that the real chimp attack was not comic to Martin Bell; nor will his face be "completely healed" until we make the movie. In the movie business, it's absolutely essential to keep believing that we will.

# 15 | NOT WANG,

# NOT WINTERBOTTOM

met Richard Gladstein, the producer from FilmColony,
in Vermont in May 1995. I liked him instantly; he was
resolutely practical. In order to make *The Cider House
Rules* "happen" as a movie, Richard proceeded as straight-
forwardly as a clock. He presented the novel and a 1992
draft of the screenplay to Miramax. Miramax optioned the
old draft of the script and the novel; they agreed to finance
the film, provided that Richard find an acceptable director.
This meant finding someone who was acceptable to
Richard, Miramax, and me. The cast had to be "acceptable" to each of us, too. That was the deal.

First of all, how hard could finding an acceptable director be? As it turned out, very.

I was part of the problem. I'm not a moviegoer, having

seen only two movies in a movie theater in the last ten years, *Schindler's List* and *The English Patient*. I saw those particular films because I grew tired of friends telling me that they were better than the books they came from. They weren't, though I thought that they were very good films.

All of the movies that Richard Gladstein wanted me to see, while we were searching for a director for *The Cider House Rules,* I saw on video. If the VCR didn't exist, I probably wouldn't see any movies. I don't like sitting in large, dark rooms with a lot of strangers. I *do* like fastforwarding through the boring parts, and being able to rewind the tape and watch again the scenes I really like. The VCR has made watching movies more like reading books.

I *used to* like going to the movies. At Exeter, I saw my first Ingmar Bergman film in the Thompson gymnasium on a Saturday night. The sound track was incomprehensible, the subtitles frequently out of focus. We sat on folding metal chairs on a basketball court, and the film was in black-and-white. But it was Bergman. Everything in my life as a moviegoer has been downhill from there.

This was what Richard Gladstein had to deal with when he asked me to "mutually approve" a director for *The Cider House Rules:* someone who had virtually stopped going to movies when Ingmar Bergman announced he had made his last film (the incomparable *Fanny and Alexander*).

The list of directors acceptable to Miramax was fairly

long, and I hadn't seen most of the movies by most of these directors. Richard's process was this: he met with various candidates, and if they responded to the material in a manner he liked (and in a manner he thought *I* would like), then he asked me to view their work. Only if I approved of someone would we move forward. It was a process that was very fair to me, but I watched a lot of movies and there were very few I liked. The list of directors acceptable to Miramax and me wound up being pretty short.

One of the directors whose work I liked was Wayne Wang. He'd directed *The Joy Luck Club* and *Smoke*. But as different as these films are from each other, in both cases the narrative is naturalistic, almost unstructured; stories overlap or run parallel to one another, but the stories are not necessarily connected to a plot. *The Cider House Rules* is a highly structured narrative, not at all naturalistic. A plot-driven story follows a predestined path. Dr. Larch's life is a plan; Homer Wells's life is designed to fit into Larch's plan.

Before Wayne Wang became involved with the project, I'd made my way through Richard's extensive notes on the script that Phillip Borsos and I had agreed to shoot. I'd already substantially revised the screenplay when Wayne gave me his suggestions, some of which were at odds with Richard's earlier notes. After my first attempt to incorporate Wayne's suggestions into the script, and in subsequent conversations with both Wayne and Richard, I found myself more inclined to follow Richard's advice than Wayne's.

I don't know if this generalization is fair, but Richard and I acted on it: if the screenwriter is taking more direction from the producer than from the director, probably there should be another director. Wayne Wang and I parted company very amicably.

The screenplay, although it now bore Richard's considerable influence—there had been much reordering of the sequence of events—remained in one respect as Phillip and I had conceived it. There was *no* Homer-Candy-Wally triangle. Richard and I had given Homer a lengthy sexual escapade (with Debra Pettigrew, one of the apple-mart women), but Homer was nonetheless a boy without a love story when he returned to the orphanage at St. Cloud's. It was still, to a degree, what Phillip and I had called "the bleak version."

And there was still no director for the movie. I remember telling Richard that I wished *he* could direct the picture; I truly wanted him to. But Richard was a good producer; he knew which hat to wear. Hence Michael Winterbottom became the third director for *The Cider House Rules*.

Winterbottom had impressed both Richard and me with his treatment of the Thomas Hardy novel *Jude the Obscure*—not the easiest of Hardy's novels to turn into a film. With the exception of Polanski's *Tess,* most of Hardy's novels that have been made into movies have proved themselves to be unyielding to the form. To Thomas Hardy, the degree of predestination in *The Cider House Rules* would have seemed mild.

Hardy insisted that a novel had to be a better story than something you might happen upon in a newspaper. He meant "better" in every way: bigger, more complex, more interconnected, and also having a kind of symmetry—at the very least, closure. His novels achieve a universal unfairness that seems inevitable. They are not just plot-driven; they are guided by the characters' fate.

Winterbottom's *Jude* captured that, and Winterbottom also made Jude's intellectual suffering emotional. As for what Winterbottom could draw out of his actors, one needs only to look at Kate Winslet's striking performance—in particular, her giving birth and her reaction to her slain children. Moreover, Winterbottom was able to capture the atmosphere of Hardy's fictional Wessex; the film looked authentic.

A director's ability to handle both the historical period and the atmospheric detail was essential to *The Cider House Rules,* wherein the claustrophobia of the orphanage at St. Cloud's, and the cider house, where the migrant pickers live, must be seen in juxtaposition to the beauty of the Maine coast and the palpable comforts of the homes where Wally and Candy come from. That Winterbottom could grasp the destiny which Larch creates for Homer was something I accepted from the moment I saw *Jude;* Winterbottom had already grasped Thomas Hardy.

I met Michael Winterbottom in Amsterdam, where I was doing research in the red-light district for *A Widow for One Year*. I was spending my days with Margot Alvarez, a former prostitute who was then the director of a prostitutes' rights organization, and my nights with a policeman, Joep de Groot, on his beat in the district. I was exhausted.

Winterbottom wasn't in much better shape than I was. It had been difficult for us to meet because he was editing his Sarajevo film, and he could spend only one night in Amsterdam because he had to be back in England for one of his children's birthdays in the morning. To make matters worse, the one night when Winterbottom could be in Amsterdam, I wasn't available for dinner; I had previously arranged with Joep to take some notes on the inner workings of a Thai massage parlor.

It was already ten o'clock at night when I met Winterbottom, with Richard Gladstein, in the bar of the Grand. Winterbottom was drinking what looked like orange juice, but—as Janet informed me later—I was half-plastered. I'd had only a modest amount of wine with dinner; yet later, in the Thai massage parlor, Joep had persuaded me to drink a couple of beers.

Doubtless Michael Winterbottom would agree: our first meeting was less than promising. Winterbottom took a back-to-the-book approach to the existing screenplay. While it is hard for a novelist to argue that any reader could love a novel too much, Winterbottom's principal passion for *The Cider House Rules* was directed toward a part of the book I had left out of the film. The Homer-Candy-Wally triangle meant everything to him; he simply couldn't make the movie without that triangle, he said.

Without it, Winterbottom argued, Homer's departure from St. Cloud's and his return to his predestined duties at the orphanage hospital would mean less. I argued that, given the time constraints inherent in a film, the love story would detract from the more important relationships—Dr. Larch's estranged but loving relationship with Homer and Homer's subsequent decision to perform abortions *because of* his discovery of the relationship between Rose Rose and her father. But for Phillip Borsos and me to have replaced Homer's love affair with Candy with Homer's one-sided infatuation with Rose Rose was unsatisfying—at least from Winterbottom's point of view, and I now think he was right.

Phillip and my "bleak version" may indeed have been unsatisfying as a love story; yet in our script it was clear that Dr. Larch's teaching and Mr. Rose's entanglement with his daughter were the main influences in Homer's life. In the film, I knew that I didn't want Candy to rival Larch's or Mr. Rose's importance to Homer.

If I had been less tired, or more sober, I might have

made a more truthful response to Winterbottom's vision of *The Cider House Rules;* I could have saved Michael and me a lot of time if I'd just said no. Lack of sleep and too much alcohol affect people differently. Some people I know become increasingly argumentative. Not me—I become entirely too agreeable for my own good. Instead of sticking to "the bleak version" and never admitting Homer and Candy's love affair into the screenplay, I told Winterbottom that I was skeptical but that I would try it. And once that love story gained entrance into the script, there would be no getting rid of it. It would even outlast Michael Winterbottom's attachment to the project, and Michael's attachment to *The Cider House Rules* was long and rigorous; we both worked very hard to make his version work.

It's interesting that Richard remembers my first meeting with Winterbottom in Amsterdam a little differently. He says: "You guys were in *complete* disagreement. Everyone thought, 'That's that, move on.' But over the next few days, after Winterbottom went back to England, we stayed in Amsterdam; we went to a church, we looked at the prostitutes in their windows, and then you and Janet and I went to a pub. It was there that you had a couple of beers (Janet and I had a couple of drinks, too), and—after a bit of prodding from Janet and me—you agreed to give Homer a life in the middle of the story. In fact, that first meeting with Winterbottom ended so discouragingly that when I phoned

Winterbottom to say that you'd agreed to try to bring Candy into the screenplay, he thought I was making it up."

Thus, according to Richard, he and my wife convinced me to "give Homer a life." On this point, Richard's memory is probably more accurate than mine. (I was distracted that entire time in Amsterdam, because my principal reason for being there had nothing to do with *The Cider House Rules*.) And Janet's memory of that time more closely resembles Richard's version than mine. She remembers thinking that it would never work with Winterbottom; according to Janet, it was the love story (not Winterbottom) that deserved a chance. She was right.

There were problems from the beginning. Winterbottom wanted to shoot the film in the spring; he simply wasn't available in the fall. The movie's main season was the fall—namely, the apple harvest. What would we do with the fact that there would be blossoms on the apple trees instead of apples? (No one ever answered that question.) Even if we'd shot the orchards after the blossoms had fallen off the trees, and the bees were gone from the orchards, even if we'd painted green apples red, the spring in New England does not look like the fall. By the time you're picking apples, the other trees—the maples, chiefly—are already starting to change color. By the end of the harvest, the peak of the fall foliage has come and gone; most of the leaves are off the trees, many of the branches bare. Nothing remains of the spring's new green. And where would we get snow in the spring? It might not even be cold enough to *make* snow.

It seemed obvious to me that *The Cider House Rules* should be made from mid-September to mid-December, but this didn't fit Winterbottom's plans. Yet, in the compartmentalization of the movie business, the manipulation of the seasons was not my job; my problems with Winterbottom would prove to be more obdurate than the weather. Now that the Homer-Candy-Wally romance was in the screenplay, there was less of Dr. Larch and the orphans at St. Cloud's, and there was *much* less of Mr. Rose and his daughter and the other migrant pickers. I was afraid that the love story was threatening to become what the movie was about. (When it comes time to "market" the movie, I'm *still* afraid of that.)

In all the previous versions of the screenplay, Candy and Wally are simply the young couple who come to St. Cloud's to get an abortion, giving Homer Wells a ride to the coast when they leave. Wally was a small part, Candy even smaller. My eldest son, Colin, was cast as Wally. But in Winterbottom's version, Wally's role had been expanded; not surprisingly, Miramax asked for an actor with a bigger name than Colin's in the part. More devastating to Colin and me was that Winterbottom thought Colin was too *old* to be Wally. (Colin was thirty-two at the time, although he could look younger; I thought he could still play a twenty-five-year-old, maybe.) Winterbottom couldn't have a Candy who was young enough to suit him, and—in his view—Wally had to be close to Candy's age. (*Early* twenties.)

Candy's and Wally's ages became a huge problem for Winterbottom and me. (Also, including the Homer-Candy-Wally triangle meant including World War II.) In the novel, Candy doesn't want to have a baby because she's still in college and her boyfriend (Wally) is in flight school. In the screenplay, once I admitted Candy and Wally to the story, I wanted Candy to be already finished with college so that Wally could already be in the Army Air Corps; I wanted him to be through with flight school and ready to leave for the war.

Winterbottom and I never resolved this dispute. Citing too little time to find adequate locations, and no actor of sufficient renown available to play Dr. Larch, Miramax postponed the planned production of *The Cider House Rules* in April 1997; they wanted Winterbottom to forgo his previous commitment and make the film that fall instead. Winterbottom refused.

Richard invited me to choose a new director. To my surprise, and Richard's, I declined. Despite the problems between us, Winterbottom and I had come a long way together on the screenplay. I couldn't bear beginning that process with someone else. Once more, I must have been tired or distracted (or both); I was again too agreeable for my own good.

As the spring of 1998 approached, Winterbottom admitted to unsolvable problems in the script and with me; he suggested that only a film in three parts could do justice to the novel, and he thought another writer should be "brought in." I had heard the film-in-*two*-parts idea before, from Tony Richardson. Now Michael Winterbottom wanted to make a movie in *three*!

I believe that, from Winterbottom's point of view, working with me was the principal problem. (Winterbottom had implied to Richard that working with Thomas Hardy was easier.) Perhaps Winterbottom had always wanted to "bring in" another writer. Frankly, I was tempted to let him. I could have written another novel in the time I had given to my screenplay of *The Cider House Rules,* and to three different directors. But precisely because of how hard I had worked to make a movie of this novel, I couldn't walk away from it and let someone else finish the job.

Also, there was Phillip Borsos to remember. Had Phillip been alive to see how the script had changed, he might have been appalled; he surely would have had trouble recognizing it. Nevertheless, Phillip would have been disappointed in me if I'd walked away. Phillip was no quitter.

Thus Michael Winterbottom and I parted company, and Richard Gladstein and I were back to where we'd been before—looking for a director. Number four. I had never heard Richard sound so depressed. At the time, what depressed me more was a foregone conclusion: whenever *The Cider House Rules* was finally made into a movie, if ever, my son Colin really *would be* too old to play Wally. That opportunity had been lost; with it I lost a sizable part of my love for the project.

# 16 | LOSING WALLY, KEEPING CANDY

hile everything was difficult, even tortured, about my first meeting with Michael Winterbottom, my first meeting with Lasse Hallström was sublime. In the script that had passed last through Winterbottom's hands, Lasse said what he missed most of all was the novel's "epic" quality; even the barest traces of the passage of time had been eliminated.

To play the history of Homer's failed adoptions as a montage, over which would run the opening credits, was (as I've said) Leslie Holleran's idea. Similarly, Lasse preferred that Homer stay away from St. Cloud's—that he not return to the orphanage—for at least a year. Between two apple harvests, Lasse suggested, we could keep alive Larch's argument with Homer, and Homer's increasing involvement with Candy, by means of another montage—and by using Homer's and Larch's letters as voice-over.

I completely trusted Lasse's instincts with voice-over because of how extensively he had used that device in *My Life as a Dog*. I also trusted *my* instincts with it; I had already made it integral to my screenplay of *A Son of the Circus*.

It has long been my view that the dislike of voice-over among American moviemakers and film critics is due entirely to how often the device is mishandled; it is frequently tacked on, after a film is shot, to clarify an otherwise incomprehensible story. This misuse of voice-over, as clumsy exposition, gives the device a bad reputation. At its best—for example, in *Jules and Jim* (one of my favorite movies)—voice-over is essential to the whole; there is nothing "tacked on" about it.

In our very first meeting, Lasse offered a radical solution to the Homer-Candy-Wally triangle—that is, maneuver Homer out of the triangle. Lasse felt that Wally should be a smaller part of the story. Similarly, I felt that if Homer were Wally's friend, his affair with Candy would be indefensible. (In the book, I had almost four hundred pages—about two thirds of the novel—to make Homer Wells a sympathetic character *before* he sleeps with Candy.) It was Lasse's idea, and I agreed, to get Wally in and out of the story as quickly as possible—before a friendship with Homer can develop. That makes Homer less guilty for the affair with Candy, but at what cost?

One is always asking that question in the screenwriting process. The constant burden of compressing a story means that *somebody's* character is going to get compromised. By reducing Wally's time on camera, and diminishing his relationship with Homer, we gave Homer less responsibility for the affair with Candy—that's true. But the character who gets compromised is Candy. To save Homer from the audience's condemnation, Lasse and I made Candy the guilty party.

Storytelling in screenplays follows a much more ruthless course than in novels. Homer is a more important character than Candy, and both of them are more important than Wally. Lasse and my solution was not only to reduce Wally's role and to make Candy the sexual aggressor in her relationship with Homer; we also made Candy less than entirely sympathetic. We *had* to. (The line I wrote for her, which she says both to warn Homer and in her own defense, is: "I'm not good at being alone.")

This situation—choosing to compromise one character so as not to compromise another—is something that happens in writing a screenplay and need never happen in writing a novel. In a novel, there is no reason all the characters can't be as fully developed (and/or sympathetic) as the writer chooses to make them. In a film, you're always fighting the constraints of time. There are characters who will be given short shrift. It's not a choice I like. (Another reason I prefer my day job.)

In restoring the Homer-Candy-Wally triangle to the script, Winterbottom had inflated it out of proportion. In essence, Lasse said, "Lose Wally, keep Candy." What happens then between Homer and Candy is a love affair but not a love story. Candy is wrong to have the affair. From the beginning, she's the one to blame.

The casting was crucial. Wally (Paul Rudd) had to be the quintessential nice guy, but he also had to have the reckless stuff from which heroes are made. He is not quite the dashingly handsome figure that Wally is in the book, nor does he possess even the potential to become Homer's best friend; yet, as in the novel, Wally is a decent-minded young patrician who can be patronizing without ever intending to give offense. Wally is a basically likable, worldly, adventure-seeking young man.

Homer is a likable, innocent, inward-looking boy. To Candy, Homer is safe. She's not in danger of terminally losing herself to him; she knows that Homer can never threaten her love for Wally. If in no way a "bitch"—and she is never calculating—Candy is nonetheless self-serving. And, at least to Homer, she is an older woman; she's the one in charge. (It helped us to find an actress for Candy who not only looked older than the actor we chose for Homer—she was physically bigger, too.)

Homer (Tobey Maguire) had to look like a kid next to Wally. Next to Candy (Charlize Theron), Homer looks like a *scruffy* kid—like no one she would ever look at twice. From the beginning, Homer must seem an unlikely replacement for Wally. (The only person Homer should seem likely to replace is Dr. Larch.)

When I first met Tobey and Paul—they came to dinner together—I was alarmed; they *both* seemed like kids to me. (Of course this was my problem; it isn't their fault that I have children older than they are.)

As for "scruffy," Paul looked scruffier than Tobey. He had long hair and a beard at the time; the people in makeup hadn't yet made him look like Lieutenant (soon-to-be Captain) Worthington. Tobey was in the company of an attractive, sophisticated girlfriend; he hardly seemed innocent, and he was clearly no orphan. But as soon as I saw them in their respective roles, Tobey *was* Homer—both an innocent and an orphan—and Paul was exactly the good-guy type that Lasse and I were looking for: the daring pilot, a leader of men.

In the movie, the main thing about Wally is that he isn't there much; even his heroism happens offscreen. The details of Wally's plane being shot down, and of his escape from Burma, are reported by Major Winslow (Colin Irving) with an uneasy combination of military precision and concern for Wally's family; and the details of Wally contracting encephalitis, and his subsequent paralysis, are likewise delivered by the major with an equally uncomfortable combination of medical detachment and guilt. Possibly the major has seen his share of combat and has escaped unharmed;

or else his aura of guilt comes from the fact that he's always played a noncombat role in the casualty branch—he may not have seen any action at all. Regardless, the effect of the major's report on Candy—given *her* guilt for the love affair with Homer—is devastating.

Major Winslow represents a kind of grown-up Wally; he is a vision of the returning hero Wally might have been. But the major is not only an older version of Wally; he's Wally with no more fooling around. Major Winslow is all business. We get the feeling that Candy likes all business; Wally's boyishness irritates her. Homer may be younger and less experienced than Wally in many ways—Homer really *is* a boy—but Homer is not "boyish." Homer Wells is all business, too; he's a very serious boy.

In the novel, we get to see Wally's heroism in Burma. In the film, we only get to see him come back, a very brief glimpse of him, looking uncharacteristically frail in his wheelchair and surprisingly small in his clothes. For the movie, Wally's role had been so reduced that I needed to create Major Winslow—not only as the embodiment of military correctness but also as a voice and a presence that can convey the utter seriousness of Wally's misadventure. The major's news spells an abrupt return to reality for Homer and Candy.

I wanted Major Winslow to be the image of how Candy might have *imagined* Wally looking when he came back. Homer might have imagined Wally returning like Major

Winslow, too—that is, if Wally had survived the war intact. Nor was the irony lost on my son Colin and me: that Colin was now too old to play Wally made him a perfect Major Winslow. But, at thirty-four, Colin had imagined himself in the role of Wally for a decade; that he was forced to accept the much smaller role of Major Winslow was a disappointment to him, and to me.

In screenplays that are adaptations from novels, you must occasionally create new characters to represent those lost moments in the lives of the original characters—hence Buster (Kieran Culkin), to represent Homer-as-a-kid. You must also create new characters to compensate for whole characters who are missing from the script—hence Mary Agnes (Paz de la Huerta), to represent both Melony, who is such a *huge* loss, and Nurse Caroline (also missing), who is romantically paired with Homer at the novel's end.

It goes without saying that Melony is essential to the novel of *The Cider House Rules,* and she provides the narrative with more than her own unchecked aggression. When Homer leaves the orphanage with Wally and Candy, he betrays Melony. She searches for him for the rest of the novel; when she finds him, she is disgusted with how he's turned out (trapped, as he is, in the unwholesome triangle between Wally and Candy).

Melony instantly recognizes that the child Homer and Candy have "adopted" is actually their own. She manages to make Homer so ashamed of himself that she is also a precipitating reason for his return to St. Cloud's. Melony is the one who confronts Homer Wells with the fact that he has *not* become the hero of his own life. "I had you figured all wrong," she tells Homer. "I somehow thought you'd end up doin' somethin' better than ballin' a poor cripple's wife and pretendin' your own child ain't your own."

In the film, without Melony to tell him where he's gone wrong, Homer Wells has to become the hero of his own life on his own. Mary Agnes can never replace Melony— no one can. Mary Agnes can (and does) do a better job of replacing Nurse Caroline.

When we first see Mary Agnes in the movie, she wants Homer to examine her tongue; maybe she bit it kissing someone, she says. Maybe you bit it in your sleep, Homer tells her—not responding to her come-on. Maybe I bit it while I was *dreaming* about kissing someone, Mary Agnes says. But more about Mary Agnes later. In casting, in order of importance, after Homer and Larch, Candy came next.

When I first met Charlize Theron, our unfaithful Candy, the line I wrote for her seemed as natural a part of her as her lipstick. If a stranger who looked like Charlize were to come up to a young man at a party, and if she said, "I'm not good at being alone," well, there aren't many young men who wouldn't instantly comply. Most young men I know would follow at her hip as dutifully as her shadow.

In the movie, Candy never stops loving Wally; she just can't stand worrying about him. Being with Homer helps Candy not to think about Wally away at the war. What Lasse understood about the Homer-Candy-Wally situation was not only that it shouldn't overshadow Homer's relationship with Dr. Larch or Homer's discovery of Mr. Rose's relationship with his daughter; Lasse also knew that Homer's love affair with Candy was not a true romance. Only in Homer's eyes does his relationship with Candy have romantic potential; the audience should know from the outset that it's not going to work.

At first sight, at least the male audience will get it: *anybody* could fall for Charlize Theron. Nor should it be difficult for the entire audience to draw a medium-quick conclusion: to wit, how unlikely it is that Charlize could truly fall in love with Tobey Maguire. One glimpse at the two of them together should suffice; we know Homer's going to get hurt. It sounds awfully simple to say this, but here's another enormous difference between novels and films: in the movies, what people look like truly matters.

# 17 | A TERSE SPECULATION ON THE MOVIE POSTER

I am fond of teasing Richard by telling him that if Candy and Homer (or just Candy) end up on the movie poster of *The Cider House Rules,* we have failed. The film is not about that romance—that *non*romance, as I refer to it when I'm talking to Richard. Dr. Larch, with or without Homer, should be on the movie poster. Ideally Larch should be wearing his operating gown. An acceptable second choice for the poster would be Larch sniffing ether.

Now that I've seen the movie (about twenty times), I think that Tobey Maguire's face has in it both the abandonment and the stubbornness of Homer Wells. Tobey's face, all by itself, might make appropriate poster material, too. My point to Richard is, *not* Homer and Candy's love affair—anything but that. (And not Candy all by herself, either.)

Ultimately this is a marketing matter. I had script approval, director approval, cast approval—rights not usually conferred to the novelist and screenwriter. Miramax will market the film. What ends up on the movie poster is advertising; I don't have advertising approval. I hope that Miramax will confront the abortion issue head-on, meaning that the marketing mavens won't try to put some sugar-coated spin on what the principal story is. To see *The Cider House Rules* advertised as a love story would be disappointing to me, and to anyone who has read the book.

Richard teases me in kind. I didn't make an appearance on the set when they were shooting the actual Maine locations, the coastal scenes and the lobster pound. Richard told me they got a lot of fabulous poster shots there—"naked embrace with heartfelt longing, raw sex, and related moments," was how Richard put it. (Virtually the *only* stuff they were shooting in Maine was the Homer-Candy affair.)

I deliberately avoided seeing any of the love scenes between Homer and Candy. I'd written them; I even liked them. But my nervousness about that relationship being blown out of proportion, in relation to the whole, was extreme. (I should say, *is* extreme.) The only Homer-Candy scene I watched them shoot was when they are having one of their arguments, when the relationship is breaking up— that and when Major Winslow gives them both the news about Wally's having been shot down, and Wally's subsequent disease and its effects. In short, the end of the love affair, although Homer doesn't know it at the time.

My notes to Lasse upon seeing his first rough cut of the film are also indicative of how much I didn't want the Homer-Candy relationship to overshadow Dr. Larch's and Mr. Rose's roles in the development of Homer's character. While I told Lasse that I mourned the loss of Dorothy's uterus, for reasons I've already delineated, and while I argued for reinstating the information that although Wally is paralyzed from the waist down, he can still have a normal sex life (and produce children), all the rest of my notes to Lasse concerned what could be *cut*.

Of those notes, only two suggested cuts did *not* concern the Homer-Candy relationship. I felt that the scene of Mary Agnes at the train station, when Buster asks Homer if he ever thinks about meeting his parents, and the scene when the girls at the orphanage are discussing Hazel's adoption—the gist of which is that the would-be parents should be forced to take the older children first, which they never do—could both be eliminated. (In his second cut of the film, Lasse shortened the scene at the train station and deleted the girls' discussion of Hazel's adoption.)

I *loved* the first cut of the film. It was two hours, seventeen minutes, and forty seconds long. The length was not a problem for me. Virtually *all* my notes to Lasse, on the first cut, were as follows.

Reduce Candy's dialogue while she is getting in the car to leave the orphanage after her abortion. Lose Wally's lobster joke—to Candy and Homer, when they are leaving St. Cloud's. Trim the interplay between Homer and Candy and Wally on the beach. Trim Candy's dialogue, and especially her degree of sexual playfulness—she's just had an abortion!—when she is talking to Homer and Wally at the apple mart. Shorten the leisurely shot of Homer, Candy, and Wally strolling through the orchard meadow. Soften Candy's laughter during Homer's first experience of eating lobster. Trim Homer's love scene with Candy, and/or the prelude to it on the beach—it goes on too long! Similarly, when Homer and Candy are naked in the cider house—and he says to her, "To look at you, it hurts"—cut away from the scene before Candy says, "Come here," and we see her breasts. (At least lose the "Come here.") Cut Homer and Candy playing pick-up-sticks, because it has the exact same tone as the scene when Homer gets nipped by the lobster and Candy laughs; we don't need both of them. In that vein, when Candy and Homer are sitting on the dock, after they've heard the news about Wally's paralysis, lose Candy's repetition of wanting to do nothing ("I just want to sit here and do nothing"). After Homer performs the abortion on Rose Rose, lose most of the dialogue between Homer and Candy at the drive-in; we know it's a good-bye scene just by *watching* them, but to hear so much of their dialogue makes the later scene at the apple mart seem redundant, or it gives us *two* good-bye scenes. Finally, when Homer gets that one glimpse of Wally coming home from the war in a wheelchair, reduce the eye contact between Homer and Candy—they've already said good-bye to each other.

Those were my criticisms of the first cut of the film I saw. They're small moments—delete the dialogue, omit a look, trim this, reduce that, cut a little—and they are principally moments between Homer and Candy, or among Homer and Candy and Wally.

In essence, what I said to Lasse was: Lose what you can of the love affair; keep everything else. *Don't* lose (I also told him) a single moment with Dr. Larch; *don't* lose a moment with Mr. Rose, or with any of the other apple pickers, either. In Lasse's second pass through the film, only one small scene with Mr. Rose and the pickers was cut—it was an introductory scene—and not a moment with Dr. Larch was lost. Lasse acted on many of my suggestions to reduce Candy's role in the film; he still kept more of her than I would have. But only a *little* more—a look here, a line there.

Don't get me wrong. My instinct to lose what we could of Candy *doesn't* mean that I disliked Charlize Theron's performance—Charlize was fine. She was all that she was supposed to be; indeed, to Homer, Candy is overwhelming. But the balance of *The Cider House Rules* belongs to Dr. Larch and Mr. Rose. Homer may fall in love with Candy—who wouldn't?—but Dr. Larch and Mr. Rose alter the course of his life. Dr. Larch and Mr. Rose are Homer's *destiny*.

To get back to the movie poster . . . Mr. Rose has more reason for being there than Candy does. While I would prefer Larch being on that poster, or simply that orphaned expression on Homer's face—or Homer with the other orphans—I could also be happy with Mr. Rose. But, as of this writing, I've not seen the movie poster. Candy may end up there. It wouldn't be a tragedy, and I wouldn't be surprised.

In the book-publishing business, I submit a novel to my editor. He suggests cuts, additions, line edits—none of which I am forced to accept. The copy editor tells me what's correct to say by noting where I may have deviated from accepted usage, but I'm permitted to remain incorrect if I want to. Then there's the catalog copy, and the front-flap and back-flap copy—over all of which I am given the last word.

I have approval of the jacket art, too. Of course there was an apple on the jacket of *The Cider House Rules,* and an armadillo on what looked like a gravestone on the jacket of *A Prayer for Owen Meany.* With the artist's considerable help (the same artist in all these cases), I designed the sink with the elephant-tusk faucets on *A Son of the Circus* and the empty picture hook against a bare wall on *A Widow for One Year.*

What I'm saying is, it's entirely possible that Miramax will get it right; they may well market *The Cider House Rules* both brilliantly and accurately. But, as a novelist, I am involved in every aspect of the book-publishing process—better said, I'm as involved as I want to be. I even have approval of the ads. This is not the case with the film of *The Cider House Rules,* over which—for thirteen, going on fourteen years—I have had almost total creative approval. Yet how the film will be marketed, which to a large extent means how it is sold to audiences, is out of my hands.

Imagine writing a novel and having someone else, without your approval, design the jacket. But that's how it is in the movie business. It's a waste of time to whine about it.

f, as I've said, "what people look like truly matters"—in a movie, I mean—the person whose looks mean the most in *The Cider House Rules* is Mr. Rose. I think it is the most difficult role in the film; beginning with how he looks, Mr. Rose has to be perfect. He controls the picking crew with seeming charm—actually, by the threat of violence. He has sex with his daughter, he gets her pregnant; yet he must remain, throughout, a sympathetic character. When his daughter stabs him, Mr. Rose allows himself to bleed to death so that she can get away.

American film culture is full of sympathetic villains, but they are not fathers who have sex with their children. Even if, in the end, Mr. Rose is heroic—he sacrifices himself to save his daughter—it is a role that requires great courage and confidence in the actor who accepts it.

I'd had the advantage of seeing Delroy Lindo read the part of Mr. Rose in that long-ago reading of the script in Paul Newman's living room; both Phillip Borsos and I thought that Delroy was terrific. The passage of time has only improved his appearance; he is still lean, but he has more history in his face, more sympathy.

Speaking to his suspicious picking crew about the prospect of Homer sleeping in the cider house with the black migrants, Mr. Rose says: "I guess we makin' history . . . havin' him stay with us!" Mr. Rose charms Homer. (For a while, he charms us all.)

"This here sensitive-lookin' fella is Muddy," Mr. Rose says to Homer. "The less said about that fella, the better." Muddy wasn't always "sensitive-lookin'"; in earlier drafts of the screenplay, he was huge and menacing. But Richard was so excited by his and Lasse's attraction to K. Todd Freeman as Muddy that I revised Muddy to suit the actor. Kenny Freeman is small and slight. This better suited Muddy's cleverness, because—after Mr. Rose—Muddy is the cleverest of the pickers, and Kenny Freeman is a marvelous actor.

Thus I made Peaches, who used to be small, big. He is played by Heavy D, who is big but gentle. Peaches is from Georgia, where Mr. Rose met him picking peaches. "He's still better with peaches than he is with apples," Mr. Rose tells Homer.

Lonnie R. Farmer, wise and reserved, is Hero—

" 'cause he was a hero of some kind or other once," is all
that Mr. Rose will say. Hero, who does nothing, has to look
like he could and would do something . . . if he had to. *All*
of them must have a level of mystery—not the least being
Jack (Evan Dexter Parke), who is just plain scary. "Jack
here is new," Mr. Rose warns Homer, implying that we
don't know enough about Jack.

We never will. Jack pulls a knife on Mr. Rose; while this
is foolish, we don't see Mr. Rose hurt him—Mr. Rose just
slashes Jack's clothes. Mr. Rose lets Jack know that he
*could* have hurt him. But Jack doesn't return with the pickers for the second harvest.

"He just wasn't up for the trip," Muddy says evasively.

"That Jack just never knew what his business was," Mr.
Rose adds with some finality.

Later, when Muddy warns Homer not to mess with Mr.
Rose, he says, "You don't wanna end up like Jack!" Lasse
cut that line in his first edit; it is part of the scene where
Muddy gives Homer his knife and tells him to give it to
Rose Rose. She will kill her father with it. But Lasse liked
it better that we don't even know Rose Rose *has* a knife
until after she's stabbed her father; Lasse cut the whole
scene. It was a very smart cut, I think—it enhances the
aforementioned "level of mystery" about all the pickers
and the migrant world.

Both the actual violence and the threat of violence in

the migrant pickers' lives are cloaked with secrecy, shaded with doubt. "This ain't your business," Rose Rose tells Homer, when he tries to help her with her unwanted pregnancy; yet earlier, when Homer is falling in love with Candy, Rose Rose warns him that he's in trouble.

"I'm not in trouble," Homer insists.

"Yeah, you is," Rose Rose replies. "I know when people is in trouble, and you is."

Second only to her father, how Rose Rose looks is critical. She was the last major character we cast. She needed to look like a young girl, but not too young; she needed to look like a young woman, but just barely. And given that she truly loves her father *and* hates him—given that she depends on him but that she also absolutely *must* leave him—whoever we found to play Rose Rose had to be able to act, too.

I remember talking to Delroy before Rose Rose's part was cast. He was worried. If Rose Rose looked as young as we wanted her to look, what if she couldn't act? If she could act, she would probably look too old. "It's got to be someone with chops," Delroy said.

We were lucky to find Erykah Badu; she had just the right girl-woman looks, and she had the "chops," too. She and Delroy needed to demonstrate some completely *natural* father-daughter affection before their relationship darkened and became sexual. Delroy couldn't do that alone.

There are three especially powerful scenes that depend on a realistic father-daughter history. The first is when Homer performs the abortion on Rose Rose, with her father's assistance; the third (and last) is when Mr. Rose dies. But it was the second of these father-daughter scenes—the actual reading of the cider house rules, following Rose Rose's abortion—that gave Lasse and me fits. We once had the reading of the rules on the first night Homer stays in the cider house, more than a year before Rose Rose's abortion; we also had Mr. Rose ask Homer to read them to him on his deathbed. (Mr. Rose hears the rules, reacts, then dies; it was an idiotic idea, and it was all mine.)

Delroy proposed the most interesting alternative— namely, that, to everyone's surprise, Mr. Rose knows how to read. *He* reads the rules (instead of Homer); all these years, Mr. Rose has just been pretending that he can't read the rules. His daughter is, of course, indignant. "You can read!" she cries. "Damn you, Daddy! How come you never taught me?"

But Lasse worried that it made Mr. Rose seem too cruel, and I was worried that, realistically—to be histori- cally truthful to black migrant apple pickers from the South in the 1940s—Mr. Rose probably *wouldn't* know how to read; that he'd be as illiterate as his daughter and the others.

In the novel, Mr. Rose knows how to read and write, but I had many scenes—and many, many pages—to make

Mr. Rose unique, to make him special. There is something about a movie that follows a more documentary path. Yet Delroy's point was well taken. In the book, Mr. Rose knows how to read. Why not in the movie?

Lasse and I simply liked it better that Homer was the only reader among them. In the novel, Homer never stays in the cider house; he never sleeps there. He sleeps in Wally's bedroom in the Worthington house. But in the movie, Lasse and I had already decided not to let Homer get that close to Wally or Wally's mother. We liked the idea of Homer living with the pickers. Hence Homer is the one to read the rules.

Whether Mr. Rose or Homer reads them, the principal point is the same. The rules are irrelevant. The rules are pointless. "Don't smoke in bed"—the pickers smoke all the time, everywhere. "Don't go up on the roof at night." But the pickers go up on the roof when they want to; they always have. Where are they the morning after Rose Rose stabs her father and runs away? On the roof. Where are they when the police come to take Mr. Rose's body away? Watching from the roof. The rules don't matter to them—they're not their rules.

In both versions of the scene, whether Homer or Mr. Rose reads the rules, the scene comes down to this.

PEACHES    They're *outrageous,* them rules!

MR. ROSE    Who *live* here in this cider house, Peaches? Who grind them apples, who press that cider, who clean up the mess, and who just plain *live* here . . . just breathin' in the vinegar? (*he pauses*) Somebody who *don't* live here made them rules. Them rules ain't for *us. We* the ones who make up them rules. We makin' our *own* rules, every day. Ain't that right, Homer?

HOMER    Right.

There's an uncomfortable look that passes between father and daughter in the midst of Mr. Rose's speech, before Homer burns the rules in the wood stove. The scene ends with the camera on Candy; she's uncomfortable, too. Mr. Rose is breaking the rules, but so are Homer and Candy, and so is Dr. Larch. (This echoes Larch's feelings, which he expresses to Angela, about her not being "holy" to him about the law.)

Here is an axiom of storytelling that applies to novels and films: the right atmosphere can justify, or at least make believable, any action. The more insupportable or unbelievable the action, the more vivid and accurate the detail must be. Take the apple-orchard location for the film— Scott Farm in Dummerston, Vermont. It was perfectly in-period, just right. The cider house bunk room, the mill room, and the roof—they all had to be correctly atmospheric, and they were. But the casting of the pickers themselves is where the real credibility of detail lies. Delroy Lindo was the linchpin to this part of Homer Wells's odyssey, but Delroy's supporting black cast also had to be excellent. They were.

One day on that set in Dummerston, I felt that my almost-fourteen-year odyssey to see *The Cider House Rules* made into a movie was finally complete. It wasn't even a specific scene that gave me the feeling; it was lunchtime in the big tent, where the crew ate. I was in the serving line, looking over the salad bar. I got my food and began to consider where I wanted to sit. There was Richard at a table with someone from Miramax. There was Lasse with his wife and children at another table. And then I saw them: Mr. Rose and his picking crew were all alone at one table, just the men; no one else was eating with them. I started toward them—there was lots of room for me at their table.

But they were so complete, so utterly themselves. They were in costume, of course; they were wearing the migrant rags that wardrobe had selected for them, and Delroy had his wig on. They *were* a migrant black crew of apple pickers from the 1940s, and I felt as Homer Wells must have felt when he first met them (and when he said good-bye to them, too): namely, that this was as close as I would ever get to them.

I had created them, but here they were—alone at their table, as if their lives had both pre-existed and outlasted my act of creation. At that moment, I had much more that I wanted to say to them—that is, in addition to telling them how perfect they were. And there was nothing, really, that I needed to say to Lasse or to Richard; yet I went to sit with either Lasse or Richard. (I can't remember now which; I was too distracted.)

I kept glancing over at the table of migrant apple pickers. In a few minutes, all the tables would start filling up; other actors and members of the film crew would join the black actors at their table, and that singular vision of them would be lost. But, for that moment, it was as if these migrant apple pickers existed only in *The Cider House Rules*. No one else could sit with them—no more than I could enter the novel or the screenplay I had written, or alter a word of the book I had published way back in 1985.

It is arguably the most memorable moment in my collected experience of seeing (and not seeing) my novels made into films, and it hadn't happened onscreen. It had happened, like *The Cider House Rules* itself, in my imagination.

# 19 | THE DISAPPROVING
# STATIONMASTER

e is in only two scenes in the movie, and he doesn't say a word; he's described merely as "the disapproving stationmaster," but in the novel he is a figure of dire lunacy and sorrow. He's also a minor character of mythic stupidity. I began Chapter Five of *The Cider House Rules* by describing him.

The stationmaster at St. Cloud's was a lonely, unattractive man—a victim of mail-order catalogues and of an especially crackpot mail-order religion. The latter, whose publication took an almost comic book form, was delivered monthly; the last month's issue, for example, had a cover illustration of a skeleton in soldier's clothes flying on a winged zebra over a battlefield that vaguely resembled the trenches of World War I. The other mail-order catalogues were of a more standard variety, but the stationmaster was such a victim of his superstitions that his dreams frequently confused the images of his mail-order religious material with the household gadgets, nursing bras, folding chairs, and giant zucchinis he saw advertised in the catalogues.

Thus it was not unusual for him to be awakened in a night terror by a vision of coffins levitating from a picture-perfect garden—the prize-winning vegetables taking flight with the corpses. There was one catalogue devoted entirely to fishing equipment; the stationmaster's cadavers were often seen in waders or carrying rods and nets; and then there were the undergarment catalogues, advertising bras and girdles. The flying dead in bras and girdles especially frightened the stationmaster.

---

In the novel, the stationmaster embodies a category of fearfulness that is beyond rescue; in fact, he will scare himself to death. "To the stationmaster, the notion of Judgment Day was as tangible as the weather. . . . Judgment Day was at hand (always sooner than it was last expected, and always with more terrifying verve). The stationmaster lived to be shocked."

He is afraid of everything. He especially dreads the cadavers sloshing in embalming fluid—Dr. Larch orders them so that Homer Wells can further his studies of anatomy. But the stationmaster is terrified of mere fruits and vegetables, too. "A hole in a tomato could cause him to escalate his predawn bouts of feverish prayer."

One night he sees the elongated shadows of Dr. Larch and Homer Wells stretching into the woods, even into the sky; he has a heart attack, imagining them to be sorcerers or giant bats. (Larch and Homer are simply backlit by a light shining from an orphanage window.)

However, in the movie, we never see the stationmaster's fear—only his obdurate disapproval. In one of his two scenes, the stationmaster is on hand to observe Homer's return to St. Cloud's. It's a winter day; the station platform is ankle-deep in snow. The stationmaster may recognize the well-dressed young man who steps off the train, or he may not. He may know that this is an orphan who left St. Cloud's as a boy and is now returning as a young doctor—Dr. Larch's replacement, because Larch is dead—or he may not know any of this. All we know is that when the stationmaster looks at Homer, he disapproves of him.

The first Friday in October started out sunny and turned overcast—a brisk fall day in Bellows Falls, Vermont, the location for the train station in St. Cloud's. The solitary line of tracks indicated the necessary abandonment of the orphanage. Indeed, the Bellows Falls train station and its attendant buildings showed all the usual signs of neglect; it required only some period automobiles, and of course the steam engine and the vintage passenger cars, to look like St. Cloud's, Maine, in the 1940s. (With a change of automobiles, the station was redressed for the one glimpse we have of it in the opening credits—when the period is the 1920s.)

When I arrived on the set early that morning, they'd been making snow for a couple of hours; the logs on the flatcars were encrusted with it. They were firing up the steam engine. Uphill from the shabby station, they were feeding breakfast to the extras. Most of them would be the passengers on the train—women with children, men too old to serve in the war, soldiers.

The first shot of the morning would be Homer Wells returning to St. Cloud's, looking every inch the doctor. When Homer steps off the train, only the disapproving stationmaster is there to give him a sullen greeting. It's supposed to be early November, 1944, shortly after Halloween, but there's already snow in St. Cloud's. In the novel, it's a new stationmaster who greets Homer Wells upon his return to St. Cloud's; he is the former stationmaster's "idiot brother," and he thinks for a passing moment that he recognizes Homer, but the doctor's bag fools him. In the film, the original stationmaster doesn't die.

Lasse shot the scene about half a dozen times, as the man-made snow melted and turned to slush on the station platform, and the steam from the engine billowed at the feet of Homer and the stationmaster.

I was the stationmaster. I had asked for the part. For almost twenty years, I had envisioned Homer stepping off that train and coming "home." I told Richard that I wanted to see that scene from the perspective of the stationmaster, who has witnessed so many pregnant women come to St. Cloud's and leave without their babies. Richard and Lasse, who were used to my nearly constant criticism of everything, were confident that I could be sufficiently disapproving.

As for the combination of the sunny morning turning overcast and gray, and the more gradual graying of the man-made snow, the weather in Bellows Falls was exactly as I had described it for Homer's homecoming at the end of the novel: "There was sometimes in the storm-coming air that leaden, heart-sinking feeling that was the essence of the air of St. Cloud's."

Tobey had a restrained, sly smile as he stepped onto the station platform. I thought it was just how Homer would have looked—the returning impostor. I don't know what I looked like—disapproving, I hoped. In truth, I felt elated. In the movie, Homer Wells has been absent from St. Cloud's for fifteen months; in the novel, fifteen years. But the boy who belonged to St. Cloud's had been in my imagination for *eighteen* years; he'd been a long time coming home.

In makeup, they had cut my hair to conform to a 1940s

stationmaster; they'd also powdered my forehead and nose. In wardrobe, they had fitted me to the unfamiliar uniform and cap, and the steel-toed black shoes. I'd dressed alone in my trailer, feeling as I once had when I'd put on a rented tuxedo for my first formal dance.

You will not recognize me; I'm not in any close-ups. You may not even be aware of the stationmaster's disapproval. I just wanted to be there, in the stationmaster's wretched persona, to see Homer get off that train.

It was growing dark when I went to my trailer and took off my costume. I neatly hung the stationmaster's uniform in the trailer closet, as if in anticipation of a second stationmaster—perhaps the real one, needing his uniform back, unwrinkled. I dressed in my own clothes and crossed the train tracks to the parking lot; by then I could see lights in the other trailers.

It was dark as I drove home. (I live about an hour from Bellows Falls.) Leaves were already falling, although it was only the second day of October. Tomorrow would be my son Everett's seventh birthday; he was not even half as old as *The Cider House Rules*. I hadn't even met Everett's mother when Homer Wells first tried to leave and then came back to St. Cloud's.

is full name is Fuzzy Stone. In the book, he's nine, in the film, six. He lives virtually imprisoned in a humidified tent, his breathing apparatus a contraption that Dr. Larch has constructed with a water-wheel and a fan; it is powered by a car battery. Fuzzy has been born prematurely; his lungs have never adequately developed. The only "developed" thing about him are his bronchial infections, which are continual. According to Larch, Fuzzy is "susceptible to every damn thing that comes along."

In the novel, I wrote: "In the daylight Fuzzy seemed almost transparent, as if—if you held him up to a bright enough source of light—you could see right through him, see all his frail organs working to save him."

But Fuzzy can't be saved, and Dr. Larch knows it. In the novel, Fuzzy dies while Homer is still at the orphanage; Fuzzy's death breaks Homer's heart. In the film, Fuzzy dies after Homer has left St. Cloud's—it was Larch's heart that I wanted to break.

The night Fuzzy dies, Larch is showing him the movie *King Kong*—a private screening in the orphanage dining room. The film breaks in the predictable place, where it always breaks, which usually elicits an argument between Homer and Dr. Larch. (Homer calls it Larch's splice, Larch calls it Homer's.) But there's no argument this time. Homer is gone. Larch is alone with Fuzzy, who loves King Kong because he believes the giant ape thinks Fay Wray is his mother.

When the film breaks, we see Dr. Larch's face in the harsh, flickering light of the projector. We see that Fuzzy's breathing tent is still—Larch sees it, too. "Fuzzy?" Larch asks. He peers into the tent. "Fuzz?"

When Michael Caine, who plays Dr. Larch, did that scene on the set of the abandoned state hospital in Northampton, Massachusetts, even the grips and the electricians were in tears. Yes, they were crying because Michael's performance was that good, but they were also crying for Fuzzy (Erik Per Sullivan); in every scene he was in, Erik was more Fuzzy than Fuzzy.

Over lunch one Sunday in Vermont, Michael said: "That boy is a treasure." True. He was a gift to the film.

The day after we shot Fuzzy's death scene, I saw Erik with his mother by the caterer's truck at the old state hospital.

"Mr. Irving!" he called to me. "Did you see me die?"

"Yes! You died very well, Erik," I told him. He beamed.

That was how he played Fuzzy, the dying boy—beaming.

In the novel, I wrote: "It was not until Homer Wells had some experience with dilatation and curettage that he would know what Fuzzy Stone resembled: he looked like an embryo—Fuzzy Stone looked like a walking, talking fetus. That was what was peculiar about the way you could almost see through Fuzzy's skin, and his slightly caved-in shape; that was what made him appear so especially vulnerable. He looked as if he were not yet alive but still in some stage of development that should properly be carried on inside the womb."

How similar this is to my description of a different character in a different novel, five years later. In *A Prayer for Owen Meany,* I wrote the following description of Owen: "He was the color of a gravestone; light was both absorbed and reflected by his skin, as with a pearl, so that he appeared translucent at times—especially at his temples, where his blue veins showed through his skin (as though, in addition to his extraordinary size, there were other evidence that he was born too soon)."

All writers repeat themselves; repetition is the necessary concomitant of having anything worthwhile to say. In another life, Fuzzy Stone became Owen Meany. Thus, when I saw Fuzzy die in his breathing tent, I was doubly moved—Owen Meany dies prematurely, too.

For the film, I wrote a scene between Fuzzy and Dr. Larch—the initial motivation for which was my concern about Michael Caine's accent. Dr. Larch is born in Maine, educated at Bowdoin and at Harvard, and he interns in Boston. Michael is from London. While it wasn't necessary for Larch to have a Maine accent—his education could easily have dispelled that—what if Michael's speech occasionally sounded British? (In conversation, Mr. Caine pronounces "Maine" as "Mine.")

In the novel, Larch grows up in Portland—in the servants' quarters of the mayor's mansion, where his mother serves on the staff of cooks and housekeepers for the mayor of Portland. Larch's father is a lathe operator and a drunk.

In the screenplay, I have Homer reading to the boys in the bunk room while Dr. Larch is adjusting Fuzzy's breathing tent. Fuzzy hears Homer reading that part from *David Copperfield* about little David not having a father.

HOMER (*continues reading*)   "I was a posthumous child. My father's eyes had closed upon the light of this world six months, when mine opened on it."

FUZZY (*whispers to Larch*)   His father's dead, right?

LARCH (*whispering back*)   That's right, Fuzz.

(*Close on Fuzzy.*)

HOMER (O.S.) (*continues reading*)   "There is something strange to me, even now, in the reflection that he never saw me . . ."

(*As Larch bends over Fuzzy to fix the breathing apparatus, Fuzzy whispers.*)

FUZZY   Is *your* father dead?

LARCH   (*nods, whispers*) Cirrhosis—it's a disease of the liver.

FUZZY   *Liver* killed him?

LARCH   *Alcohol* killed him—he drank himself to death.

FUZZY   But did you know him?

LARCH   Barely. It hardly mattered that I knew him.

FUZZY   Did you know your mother better?

LARCH   (*nods, still whispers*) She's dead now, too. She was a nanny.

FUZZY   What's a nanny do?

LARCH   She looks after other people's children.

FUZZY   Did you grow up around here?

LARCH   No. She was an immigrant.

FUZZY   What's an immigrant?

LARCH   Someone not from Maine.

What Lasse and I had wanted from this scene was to establish the simplest of reasons why Dr. Larch might not always have an American accent. We both felt that, if

Michael was in every other way brilliant in a specific take of a scene, it would be a shame to have to shoot another take only to get the accent right. At first, Michael didn't want to shoot the scene at all. With the professional actor's commendable bravura, he wanted to do the American accent correctly—with no excuses. He worked very hard with his dialect coach, Jess Platt, to make the scene superfluous.

It was Lasse's feeling, and mine, to shoot the scene just to be safe; it would cover an accent problem, if there was one. If Michael sounded American enough, we could cut the scene later.

But the scene has other merits. By the time we shot it, Michael was especially fond of it. This is Dr. Larch's only moment alone with Fuzzy before Fuzzy's death; not only does it set up the death scene, emotionally, but it's also a logical question for Fuzzy (or any orphan) to ask Dr. Larch (or any grown-up)—namely, did you ever know *your* mother and father? By the time we shot the scene, it seemed central to the story for reasons having nothing to do with Michael's accent.

When I saw the rough cut of the film, I was glad we'd done it. In the overall context of the movie, the scene won't make the audience think about Michael's accent; rather, it will make the audience consider that Dr. Larch is something of an orphan himself.

In retrospect, I thought Michael's accent was fine. He sounded more than American enough for me; there was even something very New England about the sarcastic twang of his voice. Nowhere is this more evident than in Larch's voice-over, which Michael performs with gusto— Mr. Caine loves voice-over. Here's an example of Larch's letter-writing voice. The letter is, of course, to Homer.

LARCH (V.O.)   Do I interfere? When absolutely helpless women tell me that they simply *can't* have an abortion, that they simply *must* go through with having another— and yet another—*orphan* . . . do I interfere? *Do* I? I do not. I do not even *recommend*. I just give them what they want: an orphan or an abortion.

In Lasse's second cut of the film—the two-hour, eight-minute, twenty-second version—he ended Larch's voice-over with "I just give them what they want." I mildly objected to deleting "an orphan or an abortion"; although the point is made earlier, I believed it was important enough to warrant repeating.

But this is the essence of why Lasse and I worked so well together. I am fond of hitting the nail on the head. Lasse likes to deflect the hammer.

Despite their many arguments, we know that Larch and Homer love each other. In Fuzzy's case, there's no arguing—both Larch and Homer just try to protect him. What does it matter that, in the book, Fuzzy's death breaks Homer and, in the movie, his death breaks Larch? Either way, Fuzzy is the necessary heartbreaker; that is Fuzzy's *raison d'être.*

"How come we get pumpkins only once a year?" Fuzzy asks Homer. "Why can't we have pumpkins for Christmas, too? We don't get any good presents at Christmas, anyway."

Fuzzy dies before Homer's return—before Halloween, too. When Homer Wells comes back to St. Cloud's, the other orphans are still carrying around their jack-o'-lanterns—just to remind us of Fuzzy.

The little ones never know Fuzzy died; they think he was adopted, however unlikely that might seem. "Why would the little ones believe that *anyone* would adopt him?" Buster asks Dr. Larch.

"They'll believe it because they want to believe it," Larch replies.

In the bunk room that night after Fuzzy's death, it is Buster who convinces the younger boys to believe this.

151A  INT. ST. CLOUD'S—CORRIDOR—NIGHT
(*Larch leans against the wall, covering his eyes, overhearing the boys.*)
BUSTER (O.S.)  The family that adopted Fuzzy, they *in-*

*vented* the breathing machine. It's their business: breathing machines.

(*Larch pauses; he waits to see if they believe this.*)

CURLY (O.S.)    Lucky Fuzzy!

(*Larch almost breaks with a sudden sharp breath.*)

ALL THE BOYS (O.S.)    Good night, Fuzzy! Good night, Fuzzy! Good night, Fuzzy Stone!


In the novel, it is the nearly sixteen-year-old Homer who convinces the younger boys that Fuzzy was adopted by a family in the breathing-machine business. Once again, I created Buster to compensate for losing Homer-as-a-kid from the film. But Fuzzy himself is an essential element in both the novel and the screenplay. The child who dies is the one we most remember.

Dr. Larch and his nurses are heroes, and Homer's return to the orphanage makes him heroic, too. But Fuzzy is there to remind us that St. Cloud's is not a happy place.

The last time I counted, there were 64 scenes omitted from the shooting script of 234 scenes—that is, before shooting. This means that between the March 1998 draft of the screenplay—the first draft of the screenplay that Lasse and I constructed together—and the first day of principal photography, in September 1998, we agreed to omit 64 scenes. In that same six-month period, Lasse and I added 21 scenes—one of which we later omitted. (I did not count the number of drafts of the screenplay; that might have been discouraging.)

While math was never my strong suit, it's not difficult to determine the number of scenes we intended to shoot—234 plus 21 minus 65 equals 190. But only 184 scenes were actually shot. The six scenes we didn't shoot were casualties of the ever-present constraints of time. Miramax had given us a fifty-nine-day shooting schedule; they later gave us an additional three days. Even in sixty-two days, we simply ran out of time, and six scenes were lost.

Were they important? Well . . . it's a reality of moviemaking that you have to lose something you would have liked to shoot. I've already explained that, in the novel, Homer is adopted by four foster families before Dr. Larch gives up trying to have Homer adopted. In the screenplay, largely because these adoptions take place over the opening credits, I thought that three failed foster homes would suffice. But we ran out of time to shoot the third family. The three scenes that comprise Homer's third adoption are worth showing here.

14    EXT. COUPLE #3 HOME—DAY

(*The doors opens to a THIRD COUPLE smiling at us, welcoming and embracing a sixteen-year-old Homer. Behind them waits the would-be STEPSISTER—an attractive girl, a little older than Homer.*)

LARCH (V.O.)    I told the third family to take good care— this was a special boy.

15    INT. STEPSISTER'S BEDROOM—NIGHT

(*Homer and the stepsister are in bed together. The parents burst in on them—the father chasing Homer around and around the bed, the mother beating her daughter, who covers herself with a pillow.*)

LARCH (V.O.)    It was Homer who took too much good care of himself.

15A    EXT. COUPLE #3 HOME—NIGHT
(*From her window, the stepsister watches Homer leave the house carrying his suitcase. Homer looks up at her as he walks quickly to the street.*)

The scenes aren't very significant, but the screenplay— especially given that it's my adaptation of one of my novels—is lacking in humor, and these scenes were a comic interlude that would have enlivened the opening credits and reminded my readers of the tone of my novels. I was a little sorry to lose them.

The fourth scene that we didn't get to shoot is a more serious loss. It was between Homer and Wally's mother, Olive (Kate Nelligan), eating dinner in the Worthington house. Wally is still at the war. Unbeknownst to Olive, Homer and Candy are in the throes of their affair. The apple harvest is almost over; the migrant pickers will soon be hitting the road. Homer is considering staying on in the cider house. (Because of Candy, of course.)

158    INT. WORTHINGTON HOUSE, DINING ROOM—NIGHT
(*Olive and Homer sit at the dining-room table, the remnants of an apple pie in front of them. Homer is still eating. Pictures of Wally are on the wall.*)

OLIVE    I used to hate it when Wally went back to college—even when it was just college! And that was when his father was still alive . . . I hated it even then. Naturally I hate this more.

(*Homer nods in sympathy. His mouth is stuffed with apple pie.*)

OLIVE (*cont.*)    What I mean is . . . I would like it very much if you thought you could be happy here, Homer.

HOMER (*wiping his mouth*)    Mrs. Worthington, I feel I'm very lucky to be here.

OLIVE    There's not a lot of work in the winter, and you'll have to tolerate Vernon—even Wally despises him, and Wally likes everyone.

(*Olive's thoughts drift; her eyes look up at a photo of Wally.*)

HOMER    I think Wally will be fine, Mrs. Worthington—he seems indestructible to me.

OLIVE (*distracted*)    I don't know. (*intently at Homer*) Just promise me one thing.

(*Homer is tense. Does Olive suspect about Candy?*)

HOMER    Uh . . . sure.

OLIVE    Just promise me that, if there's a blizzard, you'll move into Wally's room until it's over.

(*They both laugh, but Homer has a hard time looking her in the eye.*)


We don't need the scene for the sake of the plot. We will see Homer saying good-bye to the pickers, and we'll also see Candy come to the cider house and say to Homer,

"Olive told me. You might have told me yourself." We know he's staying. But the scene is a good moment for Olive—a complex and sympathetic character—and Kate Nelligan was superb in the role. I just wanted to see more of her.

Ten scenes later, we lost a shot of Dr. Larch at his typewriter. In the shooting schedule, the scene fell into the last hectic days, and we axed it—it seemed expendable enough at the time. Moreover, we were confident that we would find some other scene in which to use Larch's voice-over. (We did.)

168  INT. LARCH'S OFFICE—NIGHT

(*Edna and Angela view him anxiously from the doorway as Larch furiously types and types.*)

LARCH (V.O.)    My dear Homer, I thought you were over your adolescence, that period which I would define as the first time in our lives when we imagine we have something terrible to hide from those who love us.

In retrospect, I regret losing this scene more than I thought I would. It is the only scene we had of Larch at his typewriter. In the novel, he seems to spend half his life at the typewriter, writing *A Brief History of St. Cloud's.* (Naturally it *isn't* brief.) A pity, therefore, not to have one moment of him typing in the film.

The sixth (and last) scene we ran out of time to shoot is

MY MOVIE BUSINESS | 151

near the end of the movie. It is not a heartbreaking loss, and I won't bother to reproduce it here. Larch's death scene, his ether overdose, was previously intercut with two other scenes at the orphanage. One is of Buster, bringing in the wood. He smells the spilled ether, even in the corridor, and heads toward the dispensary, sniffing. We shot that scene—we had to. Buster is the one who finds Larch dead.

The other scene is of Nurse Edna getting the girls ready for bed. In the film, we see a lot of Edna (Jane Alexander); and Edna's nightly prayer, which she recites with the girls in their bunk room, plays both near the beginning of the movie and at Dr. Larch's burial near the end. At the moment of Larch's death, we didn't really need another shot of Edna with the girls, although Jane Alexander was a terrific Nurse Edna and I regret losing *any* scene with the orphans. The orphans are what *The Cider House Rules* is about; even when we don't know their names, they are often the most important characters on camera.

That was it for lost scenes. As for the other scenes I wrote—that is, the remaining 184—we shot them. As for how many of the 184 will survive the editing process . . . well, that's another matter. In the rough cut of the picture that Lasse first showed me, there were 154 scenes remaining. (That was the two-hour, seventeen-minute, forty-second version.) Not to put too fine a point on it, but as of March 1999, Lasse had already cut 30 scenes from the film.

As of this writing, May 1999, there are 151 scenes remaining in *The Cider House Rules,* and the film's running time is two hours, nine minutes, and one second. (This includes about four minutes of end credits.) I've told Lasse that I believe we would benefit from losing part of one scene and all of another; I'm also lobbying on behalf of a third scene, where I think we should put two lines of dialogue back into the picture. Whatever happens, I'm guessing that the "finished" film will have about 150 scenes and a running time of approximately two hours and five minutes—not counting the end credits.

The final cut will be Lasse's decision, and I trust him. I may disagree with one or two of his choices, but I trust his instincts. It's my job to give Lasse notes—I'm always telling him what to keep and what to lose—but, in the end, there can be only one director. Lasse is the director.

When I feel like being a director, I write a novel.

# 22 | THE TWELVE-YEAR-OLD GIRL

There is no language in a screenplay. (For me, dialogue doesn't count as language.) What passes for language in a screenplay is rudimentary, like the directions for assembling a complicated children's toy. The only aesthetic is to be clear. Even the act of reading a screenplay is incomplete. A screenplay, as a piece of writing, is merely the scaffolding for a building someone else is going to build. The director is the builder.

A novelist controls the pace of the book; in part, pace is also a function of language, but pace in a novel *and* in a film can be aided by the emotional investment the reader (or the audience) has in the characters. In a movie, however, the screenwriter is not in control of the pace; that kind of control doesn't get exerted until the editing process.

As for what novelists call "tone," the cinematography may provide a close equivalent to a novel's tone, but no matter how evocative of a book's narrative voice the camera is, it isn't the same as language.

However many months I spend writing a screenplay, I never feel as if I've been *writing* at all. I've been constructing a story—that's true—but without language. It's like building a castle (and the characters who inhabit and/or attack the castle) with blocks. The scenes are the blocks. I always write a lot of letters when I'm working on a screenplay, doubtless because I miss using language. When I'm writing a novel, I write very few letters; my language is all used up.

The moments that matter most to me in a novel are all moments of language. Here are two examples from *The Cider House Rules,* for which there are no equivalents in the screenplay. (If, in the finished film, equivalents exist, they are solely the magic of Oliver Stapleton with his camera. I had nothing to do with them.)

The first moment is a description of Senior Worthington, Wally's father—"only a tangential victim of alcoholism and a nearly complete victim of Alzheimer's disease." Senior has Alzheimer's before anyone has identified the disease.

There are things that the societies of towns know about you, and things that they miss. Senior Worthington was baffled by his own deterioration, which he also believed to

be the result of the evils of drink. When he drank less—
and still couldn't remember in the morning what he'd said
or done the evening before; still saw no relenting of his re-
markably speeded-up process of aging; still hopped from
one activity to the next, leaving a jacket in one place, a hat
in another, his car keys in the lost jacket—when he drank
less and *still* behaved like a fool, this bewildered him to
such an extreme that he began to drink more. In the
end, he would be a victim of both Alzheimer's disease
*and* alcoholism; a happy drunk, with unexplained plunges
of mood. In a better, and better-informed, world, he
would have been cared for like the nearly faultless patient that he was.

In this one respect Heart's Haven and Heart's Rock resembled St. Cloud's: there was no saving Senior Worthington from what was wrong with him, as surely as
there had been no saving Fuzzy Stone.

The second moment is a description of the cider house
after Mr. Rose's death, when the men are picking up their
few things and getting ready to leave.

At the end of the harvest, on a gray morning with a wild
wind blowing in from the ocean, the overhead bulb that
hung in the cider house kitchen blinked twice and
burned out; the spatter of apple mash on the far wall,
near the press and grinder, was cast so somberly in shad-

ows that the dark clots of pomace looked like black leaves that had blown indoors and stuck against the wall in a storm.

Most of my friends who are novelists have told me that they never know the end of their novels when they start writing them; they find it peculiar that for my novels I need to know, and I need to know not just the ending, but every significant event in the main characters' lives. When I finally write the first sentence, I want to know everything that happens, so that I am not inventing the story as I write it; rather, I am remembering a story that has already happened. The invention is over by the time I begin. All I want to be thinking of is the language—the sentence I am writing, and the sentence that follows it. Just the language.

In the case of adapting a novel for the screen, the screenwriter *usually* writes with this kind of foreknowledge. One already knows the ending; one moves the story toward it. This is the only aspect of screenwriting that resembles writing a novel for me. I know the ending before I begin; I know where the blocks go. At least that much of the storytelling process is familiar.

I must know the structure of the story I'm telling, whether I'm writing a novel or a screenplay. But there the comparison begins and ends.

The movie script of *The Cider House Rules* is a play in three acts. Act I, which details Homer's relationship with

Dr. Larch and his entrapped life at the orphanage hospital, ends when Homer leaves St. Cloud's with Wally and Candy. Homer breaks free of the orphanage and, momentarily, of Larch's moral authority.

Act II introduces Homer's new life at the Ocean View apple orchards: his acceptance by the picking crew of black migrants (and by Wally's mother, Olive); his falling in love with Candy; his subsequent refusal to return to St. Cloud's and become Dr. Larch's replacement.

Act III begins with the concurrent news that Mr. Rose has got his daughter pregnant—Rose Rose wants an abortion—and that Wally is returning from the war, paralyzed. Simultaneously, Candy chooses Wally over Homer, and Homer accepts that, as a consequence of his medical training, he has an obligation to give Rose Rose an abortion. Once Homer acknowledges her need for that procedure, he must resign himself to a broader role: he goes back to the orphanage hospital at St. Cloud's, exactly as Dr. Larch intended.

The last scene in the screenplay had to show Homer Wells not merely accepting but embracing the role of Dr. Larch's replacement. In the course of the film, we have seen both Larch and Homer reading to the boys in the bunk room—always from Dickens, and at least once from *David Copperfield,* the first sentence of which ("Whether I shall turn out to be the hero of my own life . . .") Homer finally fulfills.

I knew I wanted to have Homer reading to the boys from *David Copperfield* at the end, but there was something more important—unique to Dr. Larch. I wanted Homer to imitate Larch's blessing to the boys, his nightly benediction. That was the last scene; it shone like a beacon on some distant shore. Wherever the story took Homer, I knew where he was going to end up. In that sense, it is the most important scene in the movie; it underwent the largest number of revisions, accordingly. (Most of them concerned which passage from *David Copperfield* Homer should read.)

But there were two earlier scenes, both of which emphasize Larch's possessive love of Homer, and they were equally important to me. They required very little in the way of revision, but if (for any reason) I had been unable to be on the set for most of the shooting of the film, I would have at least made sure that I was on hand for these two scenes.

It was not until I'd seen both of these scenes shot, as I had written them, that I felt certain of the film's essential fidelity to the novel.

One morning at the orphanage, one of the orphans finds a twelve-year-old girl sleeping on the ground near the incinerator—she's not an orphan. The next we see of the girl, she's in the operating room; Edna, Homer, and Dr. Larch are attending to her. It's too late. The girl is going to die. But before she dies, she will inspire the most direct confrontation between Homer and Dr. Larch on the abortion issue.

Jane Alexander (Edna) told me that it was the abortion politics of *The Cider House Rules* that had made her want to be a part of the movie; this is the most political scene in the film.

71   INT. OPERATING ROOM—MORNING

(*Edna is holding the head of the frightened young girl. The girl is feverishly hot and whimpering; she keeps looking at her feet in the stirrups as if she's an animal caught in a trap. Larch and Homer stand on either side of her.*)

EDNA   Her temperature is a hundred and four.

LARCH   (*very gently*) How old are you, dear? Thirteen?

(*The girl shakes her head. The pain stabs her again.*)

LARCH (*cont.*)   Twelve? Are you twelve, dear? (*the girl nods*) You have to tell me how long you've been pregnant. (*the girl freezes*) Three months?

(*Another stab of pain contorts the girl.*)

LARCH (*cont.*)   Are you *four* months pregnant?

(*The girl holds her breath while he examines her abdomen; Homer examines the girl's abdomen, too.*)

HOMER (*whispers to Larch*)   She's at least *five*.

(*The girl goes rigid as Larch bends into position.*)

LARCH   Dear child, it won't hurt when I look. I'm just going to *look*.

(*Homer assists Larch with the speculum.*)

LARCH (*cont.*)    Tell me: you haven't done something to yourself, have you?

TWELVE-YEAR-OLD    It wasn't me!

LARCH    Did you go to someone else?

TWELVE-YEAR-OLD    He said he was a doctor. I would never have stuck that inside me!

HOMER    Stuck *what* inside you?

TWELVE-YEAR-OLD    It wasn't me!

(*Homer holds the girl still—she is babbling on and on while Larch is examining her.*)

TWELVE-YEAR-OLD (*cont.*)    It wasn't me! I would never do no such thing! I wouldn't stick that inside me! It wasn't me!

(*Larch, his wild eye peering into the speculum, makes an audible gasp from the shock of what he sees inside the girl. Larch tells Homer to have a look. As Homer bends to the speculum, Larch whispers something to Edna. She brings the ether bottle and cone quickly; she puts the cone in place, over the nose and mouth of the frightened girl. Larch drips the ether from the bottle to the cone.*)

LARCH (*to the twelve-year-old*)    Listen, you've been very brave. I'm going to put you to sleep—you won't feel it anymore. You've been brave enough.

(*Homer stares into the speculum; he closes his eyes. The girl is resisting the ether, but her eyelids flutter closed.*)

EDNA    That's a heavy sedation.

LARCH   You *bet* it's a heavy sedation! The fetus is unexpelled, her uterus is punctured, she has acute peritonitis, and there's a foreign object. I think it's a crochet hook.

(*Homer has pulled off his surgical mask. He leans over the scrub sink, splashing cold water on his face.*)

LARCH (*cont.*)   (*to Homer*)   If she'd come to you four months ago and asked you for a simple D and C, what would you have decided to do? *Nothing? This* is what doing nothing gets you, Homer. It means that someone else is going to do the job—some moron who doesn't know *how!*

(*Homer, furious, leaves the operating room. Edna lifts the girl's eyelids for Larch so that he can see how well under the ether she is.*)

LARCH (*cont.*)   I wish you'd come to *me,* dear child. You should have come to me, instead.

The word *tweak* is an important one in the movie business. Scenes are always getting "tweaked"; dialogue gets "tweaked" most of all. In this scene—indeed, in *most* scenes—we changed some dialogue. Edna and Larch *don't* talk about "a heavy sedation"; Larch says instead to "make it deep." In the editing process, Lasse also chose to lose the dialogue at the front of the scene—about the girl's exact age, and how many months pregnant she is—because he

Of course Larch's most important lines are: "*This* is what doing nothing gets you, Homer. It means that someone else is going to do the job—some moron who doesn't know *how!*" I thought that the camera should be on Larch when he delivers those lines, but Lasse wanted the camera on Homer's face, on his reaction. A better choice.

The girl who played the twelve-year-old was actually twelve herself. Her mother was on the set. I talked to the mother between takes. Michael talked to the girl much in the manner that Dr. Larch might have. The girl's mother told me that her daughter "understood absolutely everything" about the scene. Yet one of the wanna-be producers who'd been involved with the making of *The Cider House Rules* when Phillip Borsos was still alive insisted that this scene had to go; at the very least, the girl should be of "legal age," he said. It's hard to imagine how someone who felt that way ever convinced himself that he wanted to produce *The Cider House Rules* in the first place.

Politically speaking, if I were to make a list of people who should see *The Cider House Rules,* two groups would go to the top of the list: politicians who call themselves pro-life (meaning anti-abortion) and twelve-year-old girls.

The second most important scene to me, especially regarding Larch's love for Homer Wells, is that moment when Homer has told Dr. Larch that he's leaving, and Larch has just broken the news to Angela and Edna. In the film—not in the novel, as I've said—I imply that Nurse Angela (Kathy Baker) might have a romantic relationship with Larch, or that she might have had. Their relationship is much more physical than Larch's relationship with Nurse Edna, which is not physical at all. At least there are moments of physical affection between Larch and Angela (most notably an *ether* moment), and Angela—as only a lover or a former lover can be—is unafraid to be critical of Larch. Kathy Baker played the undisclosed sexual mystery of Angela's relationship to Larch to perfection.

But this is Dr. Larch's scene; Homer is *his* boy, and his boy is leaving.

90   INT. KITCHEN—LATE AFTERNOON

(*Buster and Mary Agnes are serving an early supper while Larch rails at Angela and Edna, who are helping Buster and Mary Agnes. The sound of children in the dining hall is intermittent and chaotic.*)

EDNA   Going where? Does he have a plan of some kind?

ANGELA   Will he be back soon?

LARCH   I don't know! He's just leaving— (*to Angela*) you're the one who says he needs to see the world! (*to Edna*) *That's* what he'll do—he'll see the world!

EDNA (*stunned*)   He's leaving . . .

ANGELA   He'll need clothes . . . some money . . .

LARCH   Let him try to *make* some money! That's part of "seeing the world," isn't it?

ANGELA (*angrily*)   Oh, just stop it! You knew this was going to happen. He's a young man.

LARCH (*almost breaking*)   He's still a boy—out in the world, he's still a boy.

ANGELA (*with sympathy*)   Just find him some clothes, Wilbur. He could use some clothes.

(*Camera closes on Larch.*)

That scene wasn't "tweaked" at all, and it survived Lasse's first three cuts untouched.

Larch is right about Homer: "out in the world, he's still a boy."

As for the ending, I can't count the hours I spent riding my stationary bicycle, looking for the perfect passage in *David Copperfield;* there were so many, any one of which could have served our purposes. We wanted to demonstrate that Homer is where he belongs; yet in the passage from *Copperfield* that Homer reads, we also wanted something that corresponds to his own life, the course of which has been marked by moments of inescapable loss, yearning, sadness.

"But not *too* melancholic," Richard warned. (Not *too* uplifting, either, I thought.)

"Something with closure," Lasse said.

The first passage I chose was Copperfield's view of Steerforth's drowned body, which has come ashore; it lies on the beach ("on that part of it where some lighter fragments of the old boat, blown down last night, had been scattered by the wind—among the ruins of the home he had wronged—I saw him lying with his head upon his arm, as I had often seen him lie at school").

One of the orphans asks, "Is Steerforth dead?"

"He *sounds* dead," Curly replies.

"Of course he's dead!" one of the older boys says.

"Yeah, yeah . . . he's dead, he's dead!" Buster concludes.

(I wanted to see Buster's face at the end—the innocent

face of Homer-as-a-kid.) But Lasse said that the emphasis on death made us think too much about Larch and not enough about Homer. I agreed.

I thought of the end of Chapter Sixty ("Agnes"), chiefly because it is so lovely—although romantic love would hardly impress the boys in the bunk room.

As I rode back in the lonely night, the wind going by me like a restless memory, I thought of this, and feared she was not happy. *I* was not happy; but, thus far, I had faithfully set the seal upon the Past, and, thinking of her, pointing upward, thought of her as pointing to that sky above me, where, in the mystery to come, I might yet love her with a love unknown on earth, and tell her what the strife had been within me when I loved her here.

But to have Homer read this passage while reflecting on his own life too strongly implies that he is still pining for Candy. Wrong.

Richard liked a passage that posed a similar problem. "Can I say of her face . . . that it is gone, when here it comes before me at this instant, as distinct as any face I may choose to look on in a crowded street?" (This passage also posed the problem that it is his *mother* Copperfield is remembering. Not good.)

I liked the title of Chapter Eleven ("I Begin Life on My

Own Account, and Don't Like It") and the opening passage
of that chapter. "I know enough of the world now, to have
almost lost the capacity of being much surprised by anything; but it is matter of some surprise to me, even now,
that I can have been so easily thrown away at such an age."
However, it fell into Richard's "too melancholic" category
to have Homer appear to be feeling sorry for himself for
being an orphan. And how would the other boys in the
bunk room respond to that? Wouldn't they just nod their
heads and look grim?

The end of that same chapter has a different appeal.
"When my thoughts go back, now, to that slow agony of
my youth . . . When I tread the old ground, I do not wonder that I seem to see and pity, going on before me, an innocent romantic boy, making his imaginative world out of
such strange experiences and sordid things!" But Lasse
didn't like the "pity" and Richard was appalled by the "sordid things," although it seems to me that Homer has been
exposed to some pretty sordid things.

"Closure!" Lasse repeated.

"There's been enough ongoing pain, hasn't there?"
Richard asked.

We had other choices, too numerous to mention here.
Finally we chose the end of Chapter Fourteen ("My Aunt
Makes Up Her Mind About Me").

Lasse shot so many takes of scene 234—I mean just the

part where Tobey reads to the boys—that one of the younger boys fell asleep.

234    INT. BOYS' DIVISION—NIGHT

(*Homer reads to the boys from* David Copperfield. *While his voice is strong—positive, optimistic, certainly reassuring to the boys—there is in the conclusion of the chapter something that distracts him. He seems to hesitate; he misses a line or two, and he appears to purposely skip one or two others. [Possibly Homer's eyes wander ahead, to the title of the next chapter:"I Make Another Beginning."]*)

HOMER    "Thus I began my new life, in a new name, and with everything new about me. . . . I felt . . . like one in a dream. . . . The remembrance of that life is fraught with so much . . . want of hope. . . . Whether it lasted for a year, or more, or less, I do not know. I only know that it was, and ceased to be; and . . . there I leave it."

(*Homer stops and looks at the boys' faces.*)

CURLY    What happens next?

(*Homer smiles.*)

HOMER    That's tomorrow, Curly. Let's not give the story away.

(*Homer puts out the lights and leaves the boys in the familiar semidarkness. Seconds later, the closed door to the hall is flung open, flooding the room with light from the hall, and*

*Homer delivers his best imitation of Larch's popular bless-*
*ing.)*

HOMER    Good night, you Princes of Maine! You Kings of
New England!

*(On Copperfield and Steerforth and Curly as the door to the*
*hall is closed and semidarkness prevails in the room again.*
*There is some giggling, some nervous laughter. Copperfield,*
*smiling, shuts his eyes. After a second, the wide-eyed Steer-*
*forth shuts his eyes, too. Then Curly.)*

*(The last to close his eyes is Buster.)*

FADE TO BLACK.


We tweaked Curly's line: "What happens next?" became
"Is that it?" (Or words to that effect.) We dispensed with
Homer closing the door and opening it again—he just delivers his blessing before he leaves—and we added an
angle of Homer in the hall, after he's closed the door. At
first we tried to end on Buster with his eyes open instead
of closed. (I've seen the ending so many times that the decision to have Buster's eyes open or closed is immaterial.)
Of course we kept the "FADE TO BLACK."

The last day of shooting, I was on the set until after
dark, but I drove home to Vermont that night; I didn't stay
for the wrap party. It didn't look as though they would finish on the set until midnight, and Richard told me that the

party would be at a bar in Northampton—a place that was popular with Smith students, Leslie said. I'm not a late-night person, and—largely because I'm deaf in one ear—parties with a lot of noise annoy me.

I was in bed, asleep, when the phone rang—it was 1:30 A.M. I could hear the music and the cheering; on the count of three, a chorus of voices shouted my name. "Irving rules!" someone else yelled. There was more whooping, and then—mercifully—whoever it was hung up the phone. I hadn't said a word.

My wife rolled over. "Who was that?" she asked.

I was already falling back to sleep, but I managed to say to Janet: "They've wrapped."

Fade to black.

© Jane Sobel Klonsky

JOHN IRVING published his first novel at the age of twenty-six. He has received awards from the Rockefeller Foundation, the National Endowment for the Arts, and the Guggenheim Foundation; he has won an O. Henry Award, a National Book Award, and an Oscar.

In 1992, Mr. Irving was inducted into the National Wrestling Hall of Fame in Stillwater, Oklahoma. In 2001, he was elected to the American Academy of Arts and Letters.

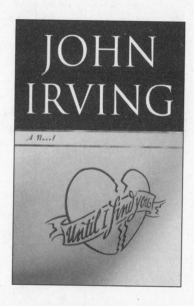

Every major character in *Until I Find You* has been marked for life—not only William Burns, a church organist who is addicted to being tattooed, but also William's son, Jack, an actor who, as a child, is shaped by his relationships with older women. And Jack's mother, Alice—a Toronto tattoo artist—has been permanently damaged by William's rejection of her. This is a novel about the loss of innocence, on many levels.

RANDOM  HOUSE | www.atrandom.com

If you enjoyed the movie, and
# MY MOVIE BUSINESS,
don't miss the novel that inspired it all. . . .

# THE CIDER HOUSE RULES

by John Irving

"AN OLD-FASHIONED, BIG-HEARTED NOVEL . . . with its epic yearning caught in the 19th century, somewhere between Trollope and Twain. . . . The rich detail makes for vintage Irving."
—*The Boston Sunday Globe*

"*The Cider House Rules* is filled with people to love and to feel for. . . . The characters in John Irving's novel break all the rules, and yet they remain noble and free-spirited. Victims of tragedy, violence, and injustice, their lives seem more interesting and full of thought-provoking dilemmas than the lives of many real people."
—*The Houston Post*

"Entertaining and affecting . . . John Irving is the most relentlessly inventive writer around. He proliferates colorful incidents and crotchets of character. . . . A truly astounding amount of artistry and ingenuity."
—*The San Diego Union*

# THE WORLD ACCORDING TO GARP
## by John Irving

This is the life and times of T. S. Garp, the bastard son of Jenny Fields, a feminist leader ahead of her times. Theirs is a world of sexual extremes and even sexual assassinations. Yet the dark, violent events of the story do not undermine a comedy both ribald and robust. In more than thirty languages, in more than forty countries, this novel provides almost cheerful, even hilarious evidence of its famous last line: "In the world according to Garp, we are all terminal cases."

LOOK FOR THE READING GROUP DISCUSSION GUIDE
AT THE BACK OF THIS BOOK.

A Ballantine trade paperback.
Available in bookstores everywhere.

"Irving's most entertaining and persuasive novel since
his bestseller, *The World According to Garp*."
—*The New York Times*

The #1 *New York Times* Bestseller

# A WIDOW FOR
# ONE YEAR

## by John Irving

"His most intricate and fully imagined
novel . . . John Irving is at the peak of
his considerable powers."
—*San Francisco Chronicle*

"A joy to read."—*Booklist*

"A wonder of a book."—*Newsday*

Look for the reading group discussion guide and
an exclusive interview with the author at the
back of this book.

A Ballantine trade paperback.
Available in bookstores everywhere.